Applied Linguistics

Stylistics, Language Teaching, Neurogrammar, Lexicography and Translation

Second Revised and Enlarged Edition

Applied Linguistics

Stylistics, Language Teaching, Neurogrammar, Lexicography and Translation

Second Revised and Enlarged Edition

R.S. Sharma

PUBLISHERS & DISTRIBUTORS (P) LTD

Published by

PUBLISHERS & DISTRIBUTORS (P) LTD
7/22, Ansari Road, Darya Ganj,
New Delhi-110002
Phones : +91-11-40775252, 23273880, 23275880, 23280451
Fax : +91-11-23285873
Web : www.atlanticbooks.com
E-mail : orders@atlanticbooks.com

Branch Office
5, Nallathambi Street, Wallajah Road,
Chennai-600002
Phones : +91-44-64611085, 32413319
E-mail : chennai@atlanticbooks.com

Printed in India at Nice Printing Press, A-33/3A, Site-IV, Industrial Area, Sahibabad, Ghaziabad, U.P.

Preface

Applied linguistics is a going and growing concern. It is a going concern not, as might be suspected, because of fad or fashion, but on account of its practical utility, its power to show results in tackling practical problems in language use and language learning and teaching. It is a growing concern because it is young and must grow; new areas of interest are bound to be perceived and explored.

Two major areas of applied linguistics are language teaching and stylistics and it is to these that this book is devoted. Although the papers collected here were written independently at different times, they all revolve around one or the other of these two areas. Evidently, the papers were not written to introduce the subject, or present it systematically. They were called forth, as it were, in response to some problems at an advanced level and, as such, they are characterized by a novelty of approach, sometimes unconventional, and, at times, by a challenging statement, which I want to explain, is not wilfulness, but a sincere conviction arising out of a thoughtful consideration of linguistic facts. Still I shall be the last person to claim infallibility; perhaps better solutions to the problems I have tackled or better analytical methods are already available. Nevertheless, it is my hope that those who are in search of materials and analytical tools in the areas of technical writing and stylistics will find in this book a good deal that is of interest to them.

As an expanding area, applied linguistics has opened up new avenues for the application of linguistic theory to real-world problems. In the second edition, besides Introduction, Neurogrammar, Modern Trends in Lexicography and the Question of Equivalence in Translation have been added. I have attempted the difficult task of keeping the new material scholarly and at the same time making it student-friendly. It shall be highly useful to students, researchers and teachers in the field of applied linguistics.

R.S. Sharma

Acknowledgements

I wish to express my general indebtedness to Professor G.N. Leech and G.W. Turner, whose work has been a source of inspiration to me and whose comments on my work have given me encouragement. I also thank Dr. R.K. Mathur for assisting me in proof correction.

Some of the papers collected in this volume were first printed in journals, others were read at seminars. The details of first printing or presentation, as the case may be, are given at the foot of the page on which each article begins. I acknowledge the sources from which the ideas have been elaborated and presented here in a book form. I am also thankful to Atlantic Publishers and Distributors (P) Ltd. for bringing the revised edition of the book.

R.S. Sharma

Contents

Preface......v

Acknowledgements......vii

Introduction......xi

Part - I—Stylistics

1. Anthropomorphism in the Language of Poetry......3
2. Metaphor: Analysis and Interpretation......17
3. Style as Artifice......26
4. Meaning and Grammar in Poetry......57
5. Language and Communication......71
6. Number in Hindi and Urdu: Observations on System and Context......76
7. Technical Style: Implications of Operationalism......83
8. Review–1 Geoffrey N. Leech and Michael H. Short, *Style in Fiction: A Linguistic Introduction to English Fictional Prose*......90
9. Review–2 Walter Nash, *The Language of Humour: Style and Technique in Comic Discourse.*......95

Part - II—Language Teaching

10. The Teaching of Technical English in the Indian Context......101
11. Teaching Semantic Distinctions Through Literature......108
12. Teaching Materials in Technical English......121
13. Dialogue and Dialogue Teaching......135
14. Teaching Poetry: A Linguistic Method......147
15. Analyzing a Poem: A Linguistic-Pedagogical Approach......159

Part - III—Neurogrammar, Lexicography and Equivalence in Translation

16. Neurogrammar....181
17. Modern Trends in Lexicography....184
18. The Question of Equivalence in Translation....196

Introduction

Applied linguistics is generally defined as an application of linguistic theory for the solution of real-world problems. We employ our linguistic insights for the solution of practical problems in such areas as language teaching, communication and speech therapy. But the definition of applied linguistics requires a lot many explanations in order to be fully apprehended. This is because there is hardly any book on linguistics which may be called completely theoretical. For examples and clarifications linguistics has to make use of real-world data. This is at least true of modern linguistics.

The most obvious case of applied linguistics is in the discipline of language teaching. It must, however, be noted that pedagogy does not depend entirely on linguistics: teaching is a composite field involving educational psychology, class management and instructional technology. Nevertheless, linguistic theory makes a very important contribution to language teaching. Therefore, language teaching forms an important sub-field of applied linguistics. There are many practical issues in language teaching which can be tackled with the help of linguistic theory. For example, the problem of grading and selection can be resolved with the help of linguistics. We can decide which structures are the simplest in a particular language.

On the basis of needs analysis we are able to make a list of the structure and vocabulary items necessary for an academic or professional sector. Linguistic analysis of texts enables us to say that the passive structure and the present tense are important features of scientific writing. Our semantic analysis shows that science depends on denotative meaning and any connotative overtones are bound to spoil a scientific statement.

An important sub-area of language teaching is error analysis. However, the impact of the transformational theory introduces a new element. The errors made by the learners in fact indicate the extent to which the learner has achieved the mastery of the system. When the child says 'mama goed market' we conclude that he has imbibed the regular rule for making the past tense. He has also mastered the rule of the transitive verb which is directly followed by an object. Even in dictionaries, verbs like *go* and *speak* are listed as irregular verbs. The learner, however, has not learnt the irregular verb forms and use of prepositions. We must, therefore, think in terms of the achievement or 'interlanguage' rather than downright mistakes. In fact, there is hardly any component of language teaching which is totally independent of the application of linguistic theory.

Another well-known sub-field of applied linguistics is stylistics. Stylistic analysis of the text can indicate the period in which the text was written, the individual style of a writer and the meaning and feeling generated by the structure and lexicon of a particular text. Let us attempt an analysis of the expression 'two wives ago'. From the study of collocation and grammar of English we know that the word 'ago' is preceded by a time expression as in 'two weeks ago' and 'three days ago'. The poet has deviated from this norm by using 'wives' which is not temporal noun. This suggests that the pressures and demands of a wife, have impelled the poet to forget time altogether. Now he measures time not in terms of weeks and years but in terms of wives. Similarly, we can say that an excessive use of the passive voice neutralizes the active force of a sentence. When Philip Larkin employs a series of passive sentences to describe the actions—drinking and act of love—which involve emotions and activity, he is suggesting the lack of activity and feeling in the modern man.

A third important sub-field of applied linguistics is the activity and methodology of translation in which equivalence is of prime importance. The same has been dealt with in a separate chapter. Etymologically, translation means transfer of linguistic material from one source language to another language called target language. There is no doubt that in modern life, translation plays a vital role in communication. Therefore, it has received considerable attention in the academic institutions and within publication industry.

Perhaps the most important theoretical contribution of modern linguistics is the phonemic theory, that is to say the system of contrastive speech sound uniquely used in languages. Therefore, the applied field of speech therapy and electronic communication must make sure that the phonemic contrasts are not obscured or completely deleted. In speech therapy, if the habit or any physiological fault in the speech organs confuses the system of contrast, then the therapist must perform surgery or administer the treatment which restores to the subject the articulation of the necessary phonemic contrast. In most languages we find oral, nasal and nasalised articulations with varying degrees of phonemic importance. For example, in French, nasalisation is far more important than in English. In English, nasal and oral sounds are kept apart and nasalisation occurs in connected speech only in certain phonetic context. Therefore, the mechanism responsible for these articulations must be properly tuned according to the language concerned.

The same thing applies to electronic communication in which the human subject is not present. In such cases the electronic apparatus used for communication must maintain the phonemic contrast. In addition, such equipment must also be geared to preserve the intonation patterns and rhythm of the language concerned.

When we delimit the scope of applied linguistics, we find that it consists of methods and technique rather than theories. Applied linguists in their respective fields are continuously engaged in developing suitable methods and technologies in their areas. For example we have a new linguistic method for language teaching and new syllabuses have been designed to fulfil the requirements of the communicative approach which lays emphasis on use rather than rule and grammar. Similarly, error analysis and interlanguage studies have developed their own methods and techniques of analyzing and classifying unacceptable utterances and sentences.

Applied linguistics is an expanding area and it has extended its scope to many other areas which may not be so important as the ones that have been discussed above. But one such area that deserves mention here is related to the field of neuroscience. Neurolinguistics seeks to benefit from the observations and experiment of neuroscience, specially the technique of brain imaging which can throw sufficient light on the locations and functioning of the brain in the process of speech comprehension and production. A separate chapter has been given on what I call 'neurogrammar'.

Part - I
Stylistics

Anthropomorphism in the Language of Poetry

Language is specific to the human species, when we apply 'language' to indicate the communication systems of bees and chimpanzees, we are already using a humanizing metaphor. Phenomenologically, language symbolically represents, or refers to, entities of human consciousness, rather than noumena or objective reality. In this broad sense, every language-act is anthropomorphic; language expresses human awareness of objects and not objects themselves, whatever their true nature.

However, it is possible to talk of anthropomorphism in a narrow and specific sense. The psyche associates certain linguistic structures and words particularly with human beings; when an attempt is made to bring a non-human object within the ken of human attribution, predication or identification, we have a case of anthropomorphism. For example, *read, brainy,* and *wisely* all have a (+ human) feature; when we predicate them of a non-human object, we are employing anthropomorphism.

Anthropomorphism has been an original means of linguistic cognition, based, perhaps, on a natural tendency of the human mind. If children are believed to repeat, at least seminally or heuristically, some habits of their primitive ancestors, we have ample evidence for this hypothesis:

Language and Style, Vol. 20, No. 3, 1987.

> The infant sees his world as endowed with energies which make him—through the phenomena of animism, anthropomorphism and magicalism—Subject and object of active processes. (Hörmann: 266)

Six-year-olds have been observed using *good, pretty,* and *happy* as interchangeable synonyms in the description of pictures (Hörmann: 282). S. Pit Corder has quoted "Table hit head" from the talk of a child (110), which is also a case of anthropomorphism.

Turning to Primitive and ancient humanity, we find that anthropomorphism played a great role in forming its conception of nature and religion. Sun, moon, sea, mountains, rivers, fire, and wind: they were all given some (+ human) and (+ + human) attributes and became endowed with a soul and volition, as well as reflective and communicative powers. It must be noted that the anthropomorphism of our primitive and ancient forebears stemmed from an unconscious drive; although it gave rise to highly poetic language, it was not the result of a conscious creative effort. But the tendency to humanize nature and religion powerfully colored the language of poetry in the ancient world. Moreover, much of ancient anthropomorphism was treated as reality and not metaphor or personification. In the Vedic period, "the gods were conceived as human in appearance" (MacDonell: xviii). The Vedic verses on Agni (or Apas) mean more than personification; they deal with real superhumans whose favours were sought through prayer and offerings—their share being the choicest of human food and drink. The same thing is true of the ancient Greek religion (and poetry). The forces of nature were conceived partly in human and partly in superhuman terms. Gods and humans had the same parentage, but their powers were poles apart. Since the skill of the metal worker was out of the ordinary, it was of divine origin and so there must be a fire god (Kitto: 54). Poseidon in the Homeric poems is more than a mere personification of the sea: he is a real god feared and believed in. Anthropomorphism of this kind continues in poetry, but with a significant difference. Forces of nature such as ocean, wind, and clouds are treated as persons with human attributes, but only for poetical effect and not as a matter of belief.

The anthropomorphic tendency of the human mind is also attested to by humanizing metaphors. Metaphor-making is a more fundamental ability than is often realised; it is part of our linguistic competence. This is why I have called metaphor a linguistic device (Sharma 1982: 29).

> Every new experience with things prompts immediately some metaphorical expressions. If some says for the first time "the brook runs swiftly", the hearer is forced by the context of "running" to forget that "legs" are originally included in the use of the world "running". (Hörmann: 226)

We do not know for how long expressions like *eye of the needle*, *foot of the mountain*, or *leg of the table* have been in use in every language. In all probability, even words like *eye*, *foot*, and *leg* originally belonged to the human sphere and were later applied metaphorically to other animate referents, and finally to inanimate ones. A study of the thousands of metaphors used in everyday language will reveal that transfer of meaning is an important linguistic means to the end of facing life through language, and it includes anthropomorphic metaphors. Poetry makes a creative use of metaphors, and poetic transfer of meaning is an extension of a general ability rather than the introduction of a new one. It should also be noted that anthropomorphism includes humanizing metaphor but is not exhausted by it, for, as we shall see, there are other ways it can be realised in language.

Now in the language of poetry, anthropomorphism has an important role because of the most characteristic function of poetic language. There are many theories about the nature and function of poetry, none of them conclusive and beyond controversy. Most of the theories, however, mention the emotive nature of poetry. Art, to quote a modern view, is "the practice of creating perceptible forms, expressive of human feeling" (Langer: 76). For Wordsworth, "all good poetry is the spontaneous overflow of powerful feelings" modified and directed by deep thinking (In Enright and Chickera: 165). This view of poetry led

> Wordsworth and later emotive theorists, through the school of I.A. Richards, to give to the nature and standards of poetic diction, or "language" the systematic priority which earlier critics had given to plot, character and considerations of form. (Perminger: 644)

Ogden and Richards distinguish two functions of words: symbolic and emotive, "The symbolic use of words is statement." In principle, two functions of words are distinct, although in language use they generally occur together. In poetry symbolic arrangements are used "for the sake of the attitude which their acceptance will evoke".

> For this purpose it fortunately happens, or rather it is part of the poet's business to make it happen, that the truth or falsity matters not at all to the acceptance. Provided that the attitude or feeling is evoked, the most important function of such language is fulfilled, and any symbolic function that the words may have is instrumental only and subsidiary to the evocative function. (Ogen and Richards: 149-50)

Richards developed this theory of poetic diction further (1924, 1929). It is, however, enough for our purpose to realise that the fundamental function of poetic language is to convert denotation into connotation: The language of reference into that of feeling and mood. It is this tendency of the poetic process that makes anthropomorphism in poetic language a central operation. Broadly, the operation consists in adding (+ human) features to non-human things and activities. It is but natural that the linguistic structures and words specifically expressive of human experience are nearer to us and touch our feelings much better than those associated with "non-human" experience. *The birds are singing* is more connotative than *the birds are chirping; the birds are producing sounds* is almost purely denotative. *The slaughtered trees* arouses more feeling than *the felled trees*. As Waldron has pointed out, in *the pelting of the pitiless storm,* "the word *pelting* attributes a malicious intention to the storm and thus arouses incipient emotions of anger and pity in the reader" (164). We shall now turn to the various ways in which anthropomorphic effects are achieved in poetry. Our examples come from English poetry, but I hope the linguistic and pragmatic categories illustrated have a universal validity.

First of all, we have to take into account the possibility of linguistic communication itself, this being a general (+ human) feature. Imperatives, interrogatives, and vocatives presuppose in the object the abilities of comprehension and response; they imply an extension of linguistic competence to the object; they have a humanizing effect, bringing the object closer to us.

(1) Phoebus, arise!
And paint the sable skies
With azure, white and red

W. Drummond of Hawthornden

It should be noted that, although the poet has used a mythological name for the sun-god, he is only conforming to the literary convention of the period and most probably does not believe in the reality of the sun-god; there is no need to bring in primitive anthropomorphism here. Anthropomorphism is introduced by the vocative and the imperative modalities, attributing the potential of human response to the sun. Additionally, the verb paint is also (+ human) (+ art). Imperatives can also be used with (– human) verbs as in

Blow, blow, thou winter wind

Shakespeare

Here it is the imperative that humanizes and not the verb.

(2) Yet once more, O ye laurels, once more
Ye myrtles brown, with ivy never sere,
I come to pluck your barries harsh and crude.

(3) Mortality, behold and fear What a change
of flesh is here!

F. Beaumont

(4) Go, lovely Rose!

E. Waller

(5) Fair pledges of a fruitful tree,
Why dost ye fall so fast?

R. Herrick

(6) Gem of crimson-colour'd Even,
Companion of retiring day,
Why at the closing gates of heaven
Beloved Star, dost thou delay.

T. Campbell

(7) Are you pale for weariness
Of climbing heaven, and gazing on the earth

Shelley

Next, we will consider what is traditionally called "personification". Abrams describes it as a figure of thought "in which either an inanimate object or an abstract concept is spoken of as though it were endowed with life or with human attributes of feelings" (62). In earlier poetry, the personified object or concept used to be written with the initial letter capitalised: this indicated that the word was to be taken as a proper noun. More important, however, is the attribution of (+ animate) or (+ animate, + human) features by linguistic means. Personification thus is the cumulative effect of many kinds of linguistic manipulation, including the ones we have discussed above and those we will introduce shortly. What is significant in this connection is that

> Psychologically and rhetorically it may be described as "a means of taking hold of things which appear startlingly uncontrollable and independent." (Preminger: 612)

(8) Doth then the World go thus, doth all
thus move!

W. Drummond

(9) Hence, vain deluding Joys,
The brood of Folly without father bred!

Milton

(10) Ruin seize thee, ruthless King!
Confusion on thy banners wait!

Thomas Gray

The following example stops short of anthropomorphism. Note how deftly the poet has attached (+ animate) features to the yellow smoke, carefully avoiding the use of humanizing vocabulary, and at the same time refraining from a direct mention of the animal. This passage affords a unique example of what may be called "linguistic felinization".

(11) The yellow fog that rubs its back upon the window panes,
The Yellow smoke that rubs its muzzle on the window-panes,
Licked its tongue into the corners of the evening,
Lingered upon the pools that stand in drains,
Let fall upon its back the soot that falls from chimneys,
Slipped by the terrace, made a sudden leap,
And seeing that it was a soft October night,
Curled once about the house and fell asleep.

T.S. Eliot

Use of pronouns (and also deictics in some languages) is also relevant to our subject. In English, *I*, *We*, *you* and *he/she* (as contrasted with *it*) presuppose common humanity as well as discoursal interaction, direct or indirect. Therefore, application of these pronouns to an animal or thing is an anthropomorphic operation. It is interesting to note that pets, personal conveyance, and some inanimate objects are often referred to by using *he/she* instead of *it*. This usage indicates a common desire to humanize the animals and things we love or which matter to us.

(12) I sit in the top of the wood, my eyes closed,
Inaction, no falsifying dream
Between my hooked head and hooked feet;
Or in sleep rehearse perfect kills and eat.

Ted Hughes ("Hawk Roosting")

(13) We shall by morning
Inherit the earth
Our foot's in the door.

Sylvia Plath ("Mushrooms")

(14) After the first powerful plain manifesto
The black statement of pistons, without more fuss
But gliding like a queen, she leaves the station.

Stephen Spender ("The Express")

Another glance at the preceding examples will show that anthropomorphizing linguistic devices are generally interdependent and they presuppose, anticipate, and justify one another. For a study of anthropomorphism in poetic language, a perceptive analysis of structure and vocabulary is required. A major source of the anthropomorphic effect in poetry is connecting nonhuman referents with vocabulary items that possess (+ human) markings of various kinds and in various syntactic relations—(+ human) as understood in the special context of this paper and not as in general linguistic analysis. We shall now turn our attention to this aspect.

We will begin by saying that in every language certain words and grammatical structures (such as the interrogative or optative) are characteristically associated with human beings, civilization, mental states, and activities—humans as contrasted with animals, plants, and inanimate objects. We are for the moment concerned with words only. As pointed out earlier, such words as *road, book, thoughtful, wise, frugally, well, think,* and *read* belong exclusively to the human sphere. We will call such words "human words" or (+ human). When a human word is applied to a nonhuman subject, the collocation produces an anthropomorphic effect.

An age old technique of poets has been to attribute a human modifier to a nonhuman object. This would be a special case of what is traditionally called "transferred epithet".

(15) Rough winds do shake the darling buds of May

Shakespeare

(16) Earth, let not thy envious shade
Dare itself to interpose

B. Jonson

(17) It is a beauteous evening, calm and free
The holy time is quiet as a Nun
Breathless with adoration

Wordsworth

Nonhuman nouns may be associated with human nouns either by compounding or in noun phrases of various types. A special case of such metaphors is offered by the Kennings of Old English poets, as when the sea is called "the swan road".

(18) And Summer's lease hath all too short a date

Shakespeare

(19) When I have seen by times fell hand defaced

Shakespeare

(20) The curfew tolls the knell of parting day

Thomas Gray

(21) Stern daughter of the voice of God

Wordsworth

The verb is the nucleus of a sentence; its semantic charge affects the other units of the sentence. That is why when a verb is used metaphorically it produces a far-reaching effect. For illustration, let us examine the syntactico-semantic properties of the verb *write. Write* indicates a specific human activity; it implies volition on the part of the doer. The activity leads to the creation of a text such as a letter or poem. We may represent its relevant syntactico-semantic features thus:

N	N
(+ animate)	(– animate)
(+ human)	(+ original)
(+ literate)	(+ human →)

(+ original) means the referent is an altogether new product and (+ human →) means it results from human effort, for what is written is certainly a human product as contrasted, for example, with a flower, which is a product of nature. Now if we construct the sentence:

(22) The sun wrote a poem (on the sky).

We are humanizing the sun and the effect is anthropomorphic (cf. 1 above). An analysis of the following examples will further illustrate this point.

(23) The fields breathe sweet, the daisies kiss our feet

T. Nashe

(24) Ruin hath taught me thus to ruminate
That Time will come and take my love away

Shakespeare

(25) The moonshine stealing o'er the scene
Had blended with the light of eve

Coleridge

(26) See the mountains kiss High heaven
And the waves clasp one another;
No sister flower would be forgiven
If it disdain'd its brother.

Shelley

Most of the linguistic manipulations described above are gathered together in the following lines:

(27) Bold foole, unrully sunne,
Why dost thou thus,
Through windowes and through curtaines call on us?

Donne

This discussion of anthropomorphism in poetic language should not lead one to conclude that there are no other ways of creating poetic effect. There are clear indications of the opposite trend, namely, conceiving human subjects in nonhuman terms. One form of this trend is collocation of human subjects with natural objects, resulting in transfer of nature's freshness and beauty to the human sphere.

(28) There is a garden in her face
Where roses and white lilies blow;
A heavenly paradise is that place,
Wherein all pleasant fruits do grow;
There cherries grow that none may buy,
Till Cherry Ripe themselves do cry.

Campion

But note the anthropomorphism in cry, which is so effective by contrast.

The other form of the opposite trend, so noticeable in modern poetry, is the conception of human beings in animal or mechanical terms.

(29) And the Jew squats on the window sill, the owner,
Spawned in some estaminet of Antwerp,
Blistered in Brussels, patched and peeled in London.

T.S. Eliot

(30) With
A single grab they have him up by the shoulders.
They dismantle him

D.M. Black

(31) ...The 'Man'
–Such was the thing called.

D.M. Thomas

Notice how deliberately the poets have chosen words with (– human) features. The modern trend away from anthropomorphism stems from modern conditions, material and psychological.

The twin factors of degraded human nature and scientific progress have combined to produce a reality that may be described as "dehumanization". Dehumanization can be viewed both as a condition of human existence today and as a linguistic device in poetry. Further, this condition has two aspects: animal behaviour by humans and mechanicalness in human activity. Each of these aspects is realised in poetry through dehumanization in two different directions. First, the language focuses on (+ animate, – human) features, both metaphorically and metonymically or, when the words are not specifically (– human), they are either suggestive of lower forms of behaviour or are associated with animals through some literary device.

(32) The silent man in mocha brown
Sprawls at the window-sill and gapes...
The silent vertebrate in brown

Contracts and concentrates, withdraws;
Rachel née Rabinovitch
Tears at the grapes with murderous paws.

T.S. Eliot

(33) The old people are terrified like cattle
rolling their eyes and bellowing, while the young
wander in darkness...

Robert Mezey

(34) We are like a lot of wild
Spiders crying together,
but without tears.

Robert Lowell

The second direction of dehumanization involves the use of metaphor and metonymy with (– animate) orientation. This leads to the generation of a multiple of semantic energies that constantly attack the potency of a human theme. I have explained this process of semantic pull and neutralization in another work (1985: 47-48).

(35) I am the cause. I am a stockpile of chemical
toys, my body
is a deadly gadget,
I reach out in love, my hands are guns,
my good intentions are completely lethal.

Margaret Atwood

(36) Being demand, I am amused
to see the centre of love diffused
and the waves of love travel into vacancy

Keith Douglas

In the last example, *love,* which has a strong human connotation, is dropped as it were, into the acid of scientific terminology; *centre, diffused, waves, travel, vacancy*—indeed, the poetic effect will be lost if we do not assign denotative scientific sense to these words. The poet has created valencies for the term love and satisfied them in a calculated way in order to drive home the idea of killing as a nonhuman mechanical operation.

Dehumanization can also be effected by grammatical means alone. A striking example is provided by the following lines by Phillip Larkin.

(37) The bottle is drunk out by one;
At two, the book is shut;
At three, the lovers lie apart,
Love and its commerce done.

Drinking, reading, and making love: these are distinctive human activities imbued with pleasure and excitement. Here, they are converted into a mechanical routine by the use of the agentless-passive, which is a favoured device in scientific language. In poetry, such passivization of particularly those verbs that take a (– animate) item as their object (such as *drink* and *read*) will invariably create the impression of "things happening", rather than of "someone doing something"—the human factor is squeezed out of the scene.

De-anthropomorphization in the language of poetry, as introduced above, requires detailed study and analysis, for it is expected to reveal new modes of sensibility that characterize modern literature.

Works Cited

Abrams, M.H. (1978). *A Glossary of Literary Terms*, 3rd ed. Delhi: Macmillan.

Corder, S. Pit (1973). *Introducing Applied Linguistics*. Harmondsworth: Penguin.

Enright, D.J. and Ernest De Chickera (eds.) (1962). *English Critical Texts*. London: Oxford University Press.

Hörmann, H. (1971), *Psycholinguistics*. New York: Springer-Verlag.

Kitto, H.D.F. (1951). *The Greeks*, Harmondsworth: Penguin.

Langer, S. (1962). *Philosophical Sketches*, Baltimore: Johns Hopkins Press.

MacDonell, A.A. (1951). *A Vedic Reader for Students*. London: Oxford University Press.

Ogden, C.K. and I.A. Richards (1923; 10th ed. 1953). *The Meaning of Meaning*. London: Routledge and Kegan Paul.

Preminger, A. (ed.) (1975). *Princeton Encyclopaedia of Poetry and Poetics.* London: Macmillan.

Richards, I.A. (1924). *Principles of Literary Criticism.* Delhi: Allied Publishers.

——. (1929). *Practical Criticism.* London: Kegan Paul.

Sharma, R.S. (1982). "Metaphor: Analysis and Interpretation." *Indian Linguistics* 43, 3-4.

——. (1985). *Linguistic Aspects of Contemporary English Poetry.* Varanasi: Academic Publishers.

Waldron, R.A. (1980). *Sense and Sense Development.* Delhi: Clarion Books.

Metaphor: Analysis and Interpretation

2

The linguistic device[1] called 'metaphor' has been the subject of wide discussion since ancient times. According to Aristotle 1920: ch. 21, metaphor consists in giving the thing a name that belongs to something else; the transference being either from genus to species, or from species to genus, or from species to species, or on grounds of analogy. He gives examples of each kind. Analyzing the last type, Aristotle says if there are four terms proportionally related then an analogical metaphor can be formed by combining two of them in the following manner:

A	B	C	D
Dionysus:	Cup: :	Aries:	Shield

'The cup accordingly will be metaphorically described as the "shield of Dionysus" (D=A) and the shield as the "cup of Aries" (B = C).'

In *Poetics,* the analogical metaphor is recognised as the most 'taking' kind. The discussion of metaphor in *Poetics* implies that Aristotle regarded it as a beautifying addition to language. In *Rhetoric,* the emphasis is on persuasion. Metaphor is a distinctive characteristic of poetry; it may be used in logical and rhetorical prose for special effect.

The classical view of metaphor is derived from Aristotle. It regards metaphor as extraneous to the basic meaning of an

Indian Linguistics, Vol. 43, Nos. 3-4, 1982.

expression: something added as adornment. The view that simile and metaphor, in ultimate analysis, are the same is also traceable to Aristotle 1924: ch. III, 1406b. The simile is a kind of metaphor, the difference being 'but slight'.

From an analytical point of view a significant contribution is made by Quintilian, although the basic assumptions remain the same. Quintilian 1920-22 distinguishes four kinds of metaphorical transference:

(1) inanimate to animate

(2) animate to inanimate

(3) inanimate to inanimate

(4) animate to animate

Philosophically speaking, Plato can be regarded as the source of the Romantic view of language and metaphor. 'One of the principles of art most clearly enunciated by Plato is that of organic unity' (Hawkes 1972: 35). This has the implication that figurative language should not be something which is added as an ornament to the thought. Plato views rhetoric from a moral standpoint. The Socratic principle underlying the *Phaedrus* is that 'virtue is knowledge, and springing from this, the main argument is that a worthy rhetoric—one aimed at the highest good—will be, not a way of fooling people in law courts, but an approach to knowledge, or an embodiment of it —a kind of inspired philosophy' (Wimsatt 1957: 59).

The integral function of language and metaphor finds its highest expression in the critical writings of Coleridge and Shelley. The poet, according to Coleridge 1962: 196, brings 'the whole soul of man into activity' by the power of imagination which, while it blends and harmonizes the natural and the artificial, still subordinates art to nature; the manner to the matter. He says (197) Wordsworth deserves praise 'as far as he has evinced the truth of passion, and the dramatic propriety of those figures and metaphors in the original poets, which, stripped of their justifying reasons, and converted into mere artifices of connection or ornament, constitute the characteristic falsity in the poetic style of the moderns'. Given the 'esemplastic' power of imagination, metaphor occupies a crucial place in the creative process. For Shelley 1962: 225, poetry is 'the expression of the imagination' and it is 'cognate with the origin of man'. Taking a Platonic line, Shelley argues that poetry affords the highest pleasure, that the cause of this pleasure is the beautiful and that poets, when they write, exercise 'the faculty of approximation to the beautiful'. The language of poets (227) 'is vitally metaphorical; that is, it marks the before unapprehended relations of things and perpetuates their apprehension, until words, which represent them, become, through time, signs for portions or classes of thoughts instead of pictures of integral thoughts; and then, if no new poets should arise to create afresh the associations which have been thus disorganised, language will be dead to all the nobler purposes of human intercourse'. Thus, in one inspired passage, Shelley has described the creation and function of metaphor and its integral place in linguistic expression.

Leaving aside the deeper philosophical aspects, we can draw certain important conclusions from the Romantic view of metaphor. Metaphor is not external to thought: instead of being ornamental, it has a corresponding meaning peculiar to it. Metaphor perceives or creates unity between disparate objects and is therefore the chief instrument of the imagination.

Hawkes 1972: 57 has pointed out that the modern approaches to the subject in the fields of literary criticism, linguistics, and anthropology have 'maintained and reinforced the essentials of the Coleridgean or Romantic revolution'. The most outstanding modern discussion of metaphor is to be found in I.A. Richards's *The Philosophy of Rhetoric*. Richards 1936 analyzes a metaphor into two elements, 'tenor' and 'vehicle': tenor is the underlying literal meaning and vehicle, the image conveyed by the word actually used. What is noteworthy in Richards's theory is his assertion that the meaning of the metaphor arises not from a simple juxtaposition of tenor and vehicle, or that of either of them, but from an "interaction" of the two. The metaphor represents a new reality resulting from a merger of the two contexts.

Leech 1969: 153-61 has tried to make Richards's formula more explicit and systematic. He has proposed a method of analysis in three stages. It is to be noted that his method is not intended to help the reader discover the meaning of a metaphor: "our task is to analyse and to explain what we understand".

In the first stage the tenor and vehicle are written in two separate lines; in the second, the two terms are completed by "postulating semantic elements to fill in the gaps of the literal and figurative interpretation; in the final stage the ground of the metaphor is stated by asking the question: What similarity can be discerned between the top and bottom lines of the analysis?"

Another noteworthy attempt to analyse metaphor is made by Christine Brooke-Rose 1958. She is concerned with studying the metaphorical use of different parts of speech and the syntactic structure of metaphorical expressions. She has discovered some important facts about the grammatical patterns of metaphors. The noun metaphors, for example, fall into five main categories.

The modern approaches to metaphor (including those I have not discussed here) certainly throw some fresh light on the nature and structure of metaphor. But they cannot claim to have made a real breakthrough in the study of metaphor. They suffer from certain drawbacks. First, they take it for granted that a metaphor cannot be analyzed otherwise than through an underlying simile; in this their view is Aristotelean. Second, they provide no help in discovering the meaning of a metaphor; if you already know it, they tell you how to make an analysis. Third, they fail to account for the impact of a metaphor. And finally, the schemes of analyses proposed by them are not quite scientific.

The most appropriate way to approach the study of metaphor is to begin with the realization that language is replete with metaphors—dead and living. Most certainly all these metaphors are not the inventions of poets. The surprising extent to which we use metaphors, suggests that metaphor is a central device of language as a process; it is a part of the human linguistic ability to deal with new experience to give a name to it.

This can be proved in several ways. First, small children when faced with a new experience often resort to what an adult would regard as metaphors. A child may find a picture 'good', 'pretty' or 'happy'.[2] Second, in the above respect, child is the father of man. Confronted with new reality or new personal awareness, men have always resorted to metaphor. 'Every new experience with things prompts immediately some metaphorical expression' (Hoermann 1971: 226). Third, it is a matter of common experience that, while struggling to express a new, complex, or unusual idea, or experience, we often find ourselves engaged in metaphor-making. On such occasions sometimes we excuse ourselves by adding such expressions as, 'so to say', 'as it were', 'as if': 'my heart jumped so to say'. Fourth, poets have always used metaphors to express their new awareness. It is on the strength of these grounds that I have called metaphor a linguistic device rather than a rhetorical figure.

Before I proceed to offer a proposal for the analysis and interpretation of metaphor, some more observations are needed. The associative tendency of words has been well recognised, for example, the association of "to fly" with "birds", and "to roar" with "lions". It is not always granted that there is also an opposite tendency to dissociate meanings of words from their contexts such that every time a certain word occurs, we do not have to imagine the context. We tend to isolate meanings in this way though the isolation may not be quite complete. Thus "to fly" means "to pass or move swiftly through air" and "to roar" means "to make a loud angry sound". Without this property of language, transfer of meaning would become impossible. Or, it would involve gratuitous and culturing "imagination". The methods of analysis so far presented by scholars insist on invoking the associations of the metaphorical words. This entails the conversion of every metaphor into a simile. Let us explain this by referring to Archibald A. Hill's interesting discussion (1976) of "semantic parallels". Hill takes two passages from Frost's poem "Bereft":

> Where had I heard this wind before
> Change like this to a deeper roar

and

Leaves got up in a coil and hissed
Blindly struck at my knee and missed.

"The question was whether 'roar' in the first passage involved a lion, and whether the several verbs in the second were a reference to a snake." The principles enunciated by Hill may or may not hold, but my contention is that reference to the associated words is not always necessary or desirable. This will become clear when we consider our model for analysis.

The model I wish to propose is based on syntactico-Semantic description of words somewhat along the lines of transformational generative grammar. For the sake of easy reference, I shall use the examples of such description given by Frank Palmer 1972: 184. Let us state the lexical entries for two words:

thought [+ N, + Abstract, – Animate]

frighten [+V, + – NP, + [+ Abstract]
Aux – Det[+ Animate]]

Now let us make a metaphorical expression:

The noise frightened the thought.

Clearly, there is a contradiction in terms of features: "frighten" is marked [– Det [+ Animate]] and "thought" is marked [– Animate]. The metaphorical force revolves on the resolution of this conflict. I suggest that the metaphor results from the projection of animateness on to "thought". The semantic transformation leads us to conceive of "thought" as a creature.

Next we will analyse a well-known metaphor, "ray of hope"

ray of	hope
+ Count	– Count
+ Concrete	– Concrete
– Animate	– Animate

We find that the last feature is common to both the words: so there is no question of transfer or projection of meaning. A [+ Count] and [– Count] combination is allowed by English in such a structure and therefore there is no conflict or contradiction. The middle features in the two columns are, however, directly contradictory. We can therefore conclude that concreteness in this case is attributed to "hope". We are forced to think of hope as a concrete object. We feel the metaphor has not yet yielded its main import. We continue with semantic analysis thus:

ray	of	hope
+ light		–
+ linearity		–

Since both light and linearity, or more appropriately linear motion, are properties of a concrete object, we cannot hope to find them in the other column. When we transfer these features to "hope", the metaphor reveals its full meaning.

We are now in a position to take up true poetic metaphors for analysis and interpretation. It will have been noticed that I have already taken some liberties with the strict transformational generative model. I must add that in our analysis of metaphors we often have to explore the semantic features to a depth seldom reached by any grammatical or semantic theory, although the guidelines are extremely helpful to a systematic approach.

The metaphors I wish to consider occur in the first two lines of Tony Connor's poem "An Evening at Home":

> Sensing a poem about to happen,
> two letters demanded to be written.

We will first tabulate the semantic features of the three verbs. "sense", "happen" and "demand" for the subject noun:

S "sense"	S "happen"	S "demand"
+ animate	– animate	+ animate
+ feeling	– subjective	+ human
– deliberation	+ temporal	+ authority

The noun subject of "sense" and "demand" is "two letters". "Letter" has the following features:

"letter"
+ Concrete
– Animate

We can now see how the poetic meaning of "letters" as organisms capable of feeling and imposing their authority is created by the use of "sense" and "demand" metaphorically. Similarly the use of "happen" with "poem" also effects semantic transformation. The attribution of new features to "poem" infuses it with a new meaning in the poem. We have to conceive of it as an event which takes place in spite of oneself: We have to class it with earthquakes, revolutions, and natural changes.

The analytical framework presented above is not complete in details and has not been fully worked out. But I think it has certain clear advantages over those I have mentioned. First, it does not approach metaphor *via* simile. We can explain the meaning of the metaphor in 'the countess sailed across the room' without bringing in 'a ship' and 'the ocean' (which is so ridiculous) by simply considering the abstracted semantic features of 'to sail'. Second, it accounts systematically for the syntactico-semantic transformations involved in metaphor. Third, it leads us to the discovery and experience of a metaphor (which is so important to poetry) instead of providing a dry rational explanation.

Notes

1. It will become clear in the course of this paper why I call metaphor a linguistic device. Traditionally figurative language is divided into two broad classes, 'figures of thought' and 'figures of speech'. Corresponding to these, we have 'tropes' and 'schemes'. Being concerned with the transfer of meaning, metaphor is a trope. The distinction between the two classes is not always clear. See Abrams 1978: 60-63, Leech 1969: 74.
2. The phenomenon has been interpreted in a different way, but what I have said about it is not implausible. See Hoermann 1971: 282.

Works Cited

Abrams, M.H. 1978. *A Glossary of Literary Terms*. Delhi: Macmillan (Indian reprint, 3rd ed.).

Aristotle. 1920. *On the Art of Poetry*. Tr. by Ingram Bywater. London: Oxford University Press.

——. 1924. *Rhetoric*. Tr. by W. Rhys Roberts. London: Oxford University Press.

Brooke-Rose, Christine. 1958. *A Grammar of Metaphor*. London: Seeker and Warburg.

Coleridge, S.T. 1962. "Biographia Literaria," ch. XIV in Enright and De Chickera, eds.

Enright D.J.: De Chickera, Ernest; eds. 1962. *English Critical Texts*. London: Oxford University Press.

Hawkes, Terence, 1972. *Metaphor*. London: Methuen.

Hill, Archibald A. 1976. "Principles governing semantic parallels", in: H.B. Allen, ed., *Readings in Applied English Linguistics*. New Delhi: Amerind (Indian reprint, 2nd ed.), 506-14.

Hoermann, Hans. 1971. *Psycholinguistics*. Tr. by H.H. Stern. New York: Springer-Verlag.

Leech, Geoffrey N. 1969. *A Linguistic Guide to English Poetry*. London: Longman.

Palmer, F. 1972. *Grammar*. Penguin.

Quintilian, Institutio Oratoria. Tr. by H.E. Butler. London: Loeb Classical Library (4 Vols.), 1920-22.

Richards, I.A. 1936. *The Philosophy of Rhetoric*. London: Oxford University Press.

Shelley, P.B. 1962. *A Defence of Poetry* in Enright and De Chickera. eds.

Wimsatt, William K., Jr., Brooks, Cleanth. 1957. *Literary Criticism: A Short History*. Delhi: Oxford and IBH (Indian reprint).

Style as Artifice

3

General Semantics

The general semantics movement arose out of efforts made by Alfred Korzybski, his collaborators, and his followers. Its origin has been traced from 1921 with the publication of Korzybski's *Manhood of Humanity* (1921). The original manuscript of *Science and Sanity* (Korzybski 1933) did not contain the word 'semantics' or 'semantic'. The term 'general semantics' was introduced by the author "for the *modus operandi* of this first non-Aristotelian system". "General semantics turned out to be an empirical natural science of non-elementalistic evaluation, which takes into account the living individual, not divorcing him from his reactions altogether, nor from his neurolinguistic and neuro-semantic environments, but allocating him in a *plenum* of some values, no matter what." (Korzybski 1933: viii). General semantics, thus, attempts a comprehensive treatment of human communication. It relates use of language to the neurological environment and makes contact with many other disciplines. The term is therefore justified in view of the approach and method developed for semantic analysis.

Two themes, however, have received particular attention from general semanticists. Their basic aim is to offer guidance and training in what may be called a healthy and wholesome use of language. It is argued that the new principles evolved by general semantics, ought to be applied in order to be beneficial.

Language Forum, Vol. 13, Nos. 1-4, 1987.

We must personally realise that the new language habits propagated by general semantics "do make our speech correct-to-fact, and that from that correctness tremendous benefits must result" (Lee 1941: 261).

General semanticists have displayed a strong pre-occupation with the misuse of language in human affairs by dictators, politicians, advertisers, writers. They have noted misunderstandings and animosities caused by wrong use of language. Writing Acknowledgements to his book *The Tyranny of Words,* Stuart Chase observes:

> The subject dealt with—human communication—has worried me for many years. I believe it worries every person who thinks about language at all. Does B know what A is talking about? Does A himself know clearly what he is talking about? How often do minds meet; how often do they completely miss each other? How many of the world's misfortunes are due to such misses? (Chase 1938: v)

After sampling the questions already dealt with by others, Lee formulates his own problems: "Why do people often misunderstand each other? How much of anything can anyone talk about? How can our language habits be brought up-to-date to fit the most advanced findings of science?" (Lee 1941: 1). Hayakawa has expressed the opinion that use of language for cooperation is "the fundamental mechanism of human survival" and that a defect in communication is the result when language is used not as "an instrument of social cohesion, but as a weapon" (Hayakawa 1952: 328).

The involvement of these writers with 'misuse of language' is quite understandable. General semantics movement coincided with and was a reaction to a period of violence emanating from a widespread misuse of words which resulted in acute suffering and death of millions of people—'fascist', 'Jew', 'communist' were used to uproot and destroy enemies, or to acquire formidable power and authority. The subversion and perversion of language have not ceased, there has only been a diffusion and subtlisation of the old techniques. It would therefore be both interesting and useful to enquire into the modern forms of the misuse of language. My object in this paper is to investigate the various kinds of misuse of style and to show by means of analysis the nature and purpose of each kind of misuse.

'Misuse', however, is an ethical and subjective term and we cannot proceed scientifically unless we first decide what constitutes misuse of language. I wish to propose two criteria, both of which must be satisfied. These are: (a) mismatching of content and form, and (b) presence of the element of cheating. Mismatching includes lack of content altogether and cheating involves an intention to gain undue advantage in terms of power, or money. If an expression is employed for a wrong content, linguistically speaking, with a view to cheating some one, it is a misuse of language. I shall now explain this notion of misuse by considering a couple of examples:

1. A and B, who are strangers to each other, find themselves together at the railway platform. They begin talking on a formal plane and in the course of discussion A insults B. Thereupon, B threatens a violent retort. Immediately A switches on to intimate style, using such expressions as 'my friend', 'oh, come on', 'you don't mean it', etc., with intonations appropriate to that style.

Now, the sudden shift from formal to intimate style on the part of A is unexpected and surprising. The style of nearness is, most probably, a hoax used to avert a consequence A himself has invited, for we cannot believe that friendship between the two can spring up so mysteriously. We have to treat A's unexpected move as a misuse of style for two reasons: first, the expressions he has resorted to, do not match with a genuinely appropriate attitude in A's mind, if he has any feelings towards B, they are not of friendliness or goodwill; second, A's change of tone is intended to pacify B by a trick of style.

2. In Act II of *Pygmalion* by G.B. Shaw, Mrs. Pierce complains to Higgins that he had been using a swear-word a great deal in the presence of Eliza:

   Higgins [loftily]—I cannot charge myself with having ever uttered it, Mrs. Pierce. [She looks at

> him steadfastly. He adds, hiding an uneasy conscience with a judicial air]—Except perhaps in a moment of extreme and justifiable excitement.

The style employed by Higgins may be called legalistic. It is characterized by the nature of modification—the adverbial clause, 'perhaps' and 'justifiable'—and by a deliberate choice of words. Higgins obviously has played this trick in order to defend himself and confuse the fact Mrs. Pierce knows too well

Let us be a little more clear about the element of cheating before we proceed. I wish to use the term in a broad sense including deception and trickery. It may be deliberate and preplanned, inadvertent, or even unconscious. We shall judge its presence on the basis of an analysis of intention, context and consequence along with the language used.

It should be noted that we are not concerned with misuse of words—but with the system of discourse: the rules of the game. This brings us close to the 'Language-games' theory.

Language-Games

Wittgenstein first proposed a picture theory of language and later replaced it by his famous game theory (Wittgenstein 1953). My present task is not to present either of these theories in their entirety. Only two aspects of the language-games theory, are relevant to our discussion.

In the first place, language-games serve as a link between language and reality. They have a philosophical import; they are not games of language, but games played by means of language. Words acquire their meanings from their role in the complex activities, called language-games, which, let me repeat, are more than games of language. According to Hintikka's interpretation, Wittgenstein regarded language-games as "the mediators between language and reality" (Saarinen 1979: 8). I take this to be an acceptable interpretation.

My point is that, although not clearly stated, one implication of Wittgenstein's idea would be that the way language is used also has a meaning derived from the role it plays in language-games. I am here trying to give an epistemic status not only to the words used but also to the style. We must, thus, assume that style also has a meaning in its own right and that different styles have different meanings according to their role in language-games. Secondly, games are rule-governed activities in fact, the essence of a game consists in the complex structure of its rules. The rules are derived from language-games and not *vice-versa*. As Hintikka has said, "it is also instructive to see what a central role is played in game-theoretical semantics by the notion of strategy (a sort of rule) for playing some particular in sense of choosing one's moves" (Saarinen 1979: 23). Wittgenstein even states that "lying is a language-game that needs to be learned like any other one" (1953: 90c).

From this discussion of game rules, we can draw certain inferences for our study. Rules of style arise out of the typical activities, e.g. arguing before a court, making a scientific experiment, selling books. You do not arrive at rules of language-games deductively. Next, game rules are liable to breach and cheating. In the use of style, too, which, we have seen, is also a matter of rules, there is scope for fouling and deception by dishonest players.

We are now, I hope, in a position to examine the misuse of particular styles, but before this is done it is desirable to be clear about the terms 'style' and 'artifice'.

'Style' and 'Artifice'

The term 'style' is difficult to define precisely. Crystal and Davy have distinguished four senses in which it has been used, including an evaluative one (1969: 9-10). Halliday *et al.* treated it as a dimension of what they called, 'register classification' (1964: 92). Ohmann has added a philosophical element to the question of style: he insists on a dichotomy between form and content, declaring that there can be no stylistics without such a division. What the style of an author does is to reveal, what Ohmann calls, his "epistemic choices" (Babb 1972: 36-49). Similarly, Epstein distinguishes between "what" and "how" which correspond to content and form respectively, with ample illustration from both linguistic and non-linguistic activities, e.g. the game of tennis (1978). Ohmann and Epstein, when they took up this dualistic position, were talking primarily of literary style, but the distinction they made can be extended to cover style in general. According to Akhmanova, "the concept of style presupposes the existence of objects which are essentially identical, but which differ in some secondary, subservient feature or features" (1976: 3). This remark is applicable to linguistic style in general, but it is not strictly dualistic; in my opinion, it also suffers from a philosophical weakness which will become clear presently. Monistic and pluralistic conceptions of style have also been pointed out (Leech and Short 1981: 14-38).

We will do well to settle this controversy in some way and evolve a view of style which covers both literary and non-literary forms of discourse and is also philosophically on a sound basis. We shall begin by saying that reality-in-itself, i.e. outside human consciousness is unknowable. So what we call objects or things, such as mountain, table, are forms of consciousness, and as such, they are not radically different from feelings, e.g. headache and concepts, e.g. height. We can, however, classify different forms of consciousness and distinguish between, say, 'mountain' and 'headache': on this basis, we can say that even the so-called 'empty words' have a reference. I have pleaded elsewhere that a general theory of reference would make semantic analysis simpler and more scientific (Sharma 1985b: 246). Now the forms of human consciousness in their totality, we shall call 'reality'. It is possible to suggest that the configuration of reality in the sense defined above is a projection of objects in themselves. This, however, is a question we shall keep apart. On the other hand, I wish to propose that reality in our sense is divided not only vertically, e.g., *earth, sky,* and horizontally, e.g. *kitchen, bedroom,* but also laterally *and it is the lateral division of reality which is symbolised by style,* whether we think of linguistic style in general or literary style, the other two divisions are symbolised by the other levels of language. This theoretical position will enable us to see, for example, how the different 'sides' of love are represented in psychology, poetry and in common parlance. Thus, there can be no piece of discourse which is devoid of style altogether, although the least-marked, namely the style of everyday communication may be called neutral, or zero-style, where 'zero' certainly has a great deal of meaning, since the distinguishing features of conversational style can be clearly identified and described.

The above analysis offers two advantages. First, as hinted above, it facilitates a general theory of style; reality is multifaceted—creative writers can always discover new and hidden aspects of things—and each form of discourse captures through its characteristic style one particular side of reality. Second, style has a content, it is not merely a way of expression devoid of any correlative in the structure of reality. It is possible for us to discover the 'referent' for each kind of style. It must be noted here that I am using both 'content' and 'referent' in a wider sense than is usually taken in semantics.

How do we discover the referent of a style? By analysing the language used at the stylistic level. This brings us to a text-oriented definition of style. In this regard, the definition sponsored by Bernard Bloch is still very useful:

> The style of a discourse is the message carried by the frequency distributions and transitional probabilities of its linguistic features, especially as they differ from those of the same features in the language as a whole. (1953: 42)

The message in this definition is to be equated with our 'content' or 'referent' of style. What I wish to add is that the linguistic features in question are a matter of choice and that they carry a stylistic meaning. Stylistic choices are based on conventions, but the conventions themselves develop in conformity with the nature of stylistic content. Style is not a matter of unrestricted choice, although the degree of freedom varies from discourse to discourse. We can represent the variation by means of a triangle:

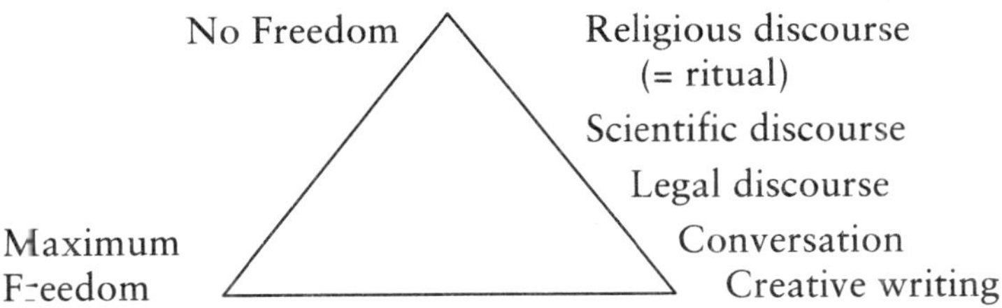

It should be noted that "no freedom" does not mean absence of choice in terms of linguistic features: it simply means that the choice is predetermined.

This discussion of style calls for a new definition of the term. I can propose only a tentative one: *style is an aspect of language-use which characteristically correlates a specific lateral meaning of reality to the nature and distribution of the words and structural units employed in a discourse as a matter of choice, and not of grammatical rule.* This definition for one thing, underlines the idea that each style has a meaning of its own, and, for another, it points to the linguistic level at which style is analysed. The other elements of this definition will, I hope, become clearer as we proceed.

So much for style. The word "artifice" has been used in one of its dictionary senses—indeed the most common one. The OED defines the word thus:

> 5. Skill in designing and employing expedients; address, cunning, trickery.
>
> 7. An ingenious expedient, a manoeuvre, stratagem, device, contrivance, trick.

Webster's New Twentieth Century Dictionary gives the following meaning:

> 4. A Clever expedient, trick, artful device.

We pick out three constituents which are common to the two sets of definitions: these are cleverness, expedient and trickery. They constitute the essential meaning of 'artifice'. Moreover, together they imply deception or cheating with the purpose of meeting a difficult situation or gaining an undue advantage (expedient). We are ready to address our efforts to the central theme of this paper.

Impersonal Style

This is the style proper to scientific and technical discourse; we shall also call it technical style. Impersonal style is distinguished by certain linguistic features: the agentless passive, functional use of 'we' and 'you', unmarked tense (past tense is used in reports of experiments), (Crystal and Davy 1969: 251-53; Turner 1973: 180-84; Sharma 1975: 8-9; Sharma 1978: 158). Writers on technical English, have often recommended a mechanical use of this style to the students of science and technology (Kelley 1972: 57-59; Sharma 1985c: 81-89). I have myself been guilty of "correcting" the language of many dissertations on scientific and technical topics in order to make them conform to the rules of impersonal style.

So strong is the weight of conventions and the authority of the handbook that it is seldom realised that the impersonal style has its distinctive content: what we have called the lateral meaning of reality. The impersonal style indicates that the phenomenon being described is independent of the observer (a view already endangered by Einstein's work on relativity!), that it is verifiable or predictable, that the description or interpretation has perfect dependability and it is an expression of fact and not of feeling.

Technical style thus makes a certain kind of impression on the reader and the reader's attitude is guided by this impression: he acts accordingly. This style has acquired great prestige and authority in the public mind and hence the need to investigate its use carefully. If impersonal style used in a text does not have its corresponding content, or is mismatched to an inappropriate content, it will cause misunderstanding and, as we shall see presently, sometimes incalculable harm. But a mere mismatching of content and form does not constitute artifice, for "stylistic incongruity can be used with deliberate effect by humorists and poets" (Lyons 1981: 294-95). Take, for example, the following lines from Zamyatin's novel translated with the title *We:*

> Eternal lovers are these Two-Times-Two,
> Forever blent in a passionate Four;

No others can so ardently adore
As these inseparable Two-Times-Two!

(Zamyatin 1972: 76)

Mark the preponderance of emotive words, personification, the poetical form 'blent', the rhyme scheme, a b b a, and metrical arrangement—all of which establish a poetic style. On the other hand the content is mathematical: $2 \times 2 = 4$. We cannot, however, regard the style used here as an artifice, because the writer has not employed it to deceive or coerce anyone.

Let us now take a reverse case. Suppose I decide to write a book with the title "The Science of Love". What I am doing is to create an impression that love can be described objectively in the form of universally valid and verifiable principles and laws. I am also claiming superiority to other writers on love. The precise semantic implications of such combinations as the above, I have tried to explain elsewhere (Sharma 1985a: 47-48). Now suppose further that I write the following:

> Let L_n be a measure of the love which a woman S feels for a man H after n months of companionship. Further, let, R_{m1}, R_{m2}.... R_{mn}, be the sums of money transferred from H to S at the end of the first, the second...the nth month.

then,

$$L_n \propto R_{m1} + R_{m2} + R_{m3} \dots R_{mn}$$

$$\text{or } L_n = K[R_{m1} + R_{m2} + \dots R_{mn}]$$

where K is a constant of proportionality which will depend on the social norms with regard to SH relationship.

This formulation about love and money is not so innocent as Zamyatin's verse on multiplication, for the language in which it is couched creates an impression that the equations presented are true in the same sense in which statements about the physical phenomena are true. Therefore, the style of the above formulation constitutes artifice—it has mismatching of content and form as well as an element of deception.

Technical style may get misused as artifice deliberately, inadvertently, or as a matter of slavish adherence to convention. In all cases it can lead to dangerous misunderstanding. The results of a scientific experiment are not always so objective, dependable and unconditional as the style makes them appear. "There is an interesting saying that no one believes an hypothesis except its originator but everyone believes an experiment except the experimenter. Most people are ready to believe something based on experiment but the experimenter knows the many little things that could have gone wrong in the experiment" (Beveridge 1950: 65). According to Conant, scientists are free neither from value judgements nor from ambition. He repudiates the picture of a scientist as a cool, impartial, detached observer. He feels there is nothing wrong in an emotional attachment to one's own point of view but it is "particularly insidious in science because it is so easy for the proponent of a project to clothe his convictions in technical language" (1952: 66-67). The point is that when an experiment is written down, the requirements of style do not permit inclusion of such expressions as would reflect the various weaknesses and limitations of the experiment. And, as we shall see, what is omitted from the language of the experiment is of vital importance.

I wish to make the above point clearer by a detailed consideration of a specific text. In 1958, a new sedative hypnotic drug was introduced by The Distillers Company (Biochemicals) under the trade name 'Distaval'. It was a preparation of Thalidomide, a derivative of glutamic acid. A report on the pharmacological properties of the drug written by G.F. Somers was published in the *British Journal of Pharmacology and Chemotherapy* (1960, 15: 111-16). I shall quote from this report:

> Thalidomide has been shown experimentally to be a sedative hypnotic drug acting differently from the barbiturates. It does not cause incoordination, respiratory depression or narcosis, and it is virtually nontoxic, possibly due to a limited absorption. The clinical value of this drug has been reported by Jung (1956), Stark (1956) and by Burley, Dennison and Harrison (1959). Its safety has been confirmed in a

> number of cases of accidental and suicidal overdoses (de Souza 1959; Burley, personal communication). (116)

It is noticeable that the unfavourable terms have been negated either by 'not' or by the negative prefix ('non-toxic'), the favourable terms ('value' and 'safety') are foregrounded. 'Experimentally' as noted earlier makes a great appeal; it is a password for dependability. The first sentence is in the impersonal passive, lending an objective force to the statement. 'Confirmed' is also highly reassuring. The confirmation of safety actually rests on reports by two doctors only, which is not at all sufficient to justify the claim, but 'in a number of cases' covers up the deficiency. 'Possibly due to a limited absorptions' is quite effective, although considering the evidence, many mute questions remain unanswered.

I do not charge the investigator with deliberate cheating; probably the style did the trick, but we are forced to do some rethinking on technical style by the terrible consequences reported later (Lenz 1962: 45; McBride 1961: 1358). The impression would have been quite different if the investigator had reported the experiment in the following manner:

> My experiment has shown Thalidomide to be.... As far as animals are concerned (I used mice and cats), it does not cause... this is perhaps due to a limited absorption. A few practitioners have reported....

I guess, many scientists will ridicule this alternative, but such a style was not uncommon in an earlier period. Consider the following extract from Newton's *Principia Mathematica* in English translation, quoted by Taylor:

> I wish we could derive the rest of the phenomena of nature by the same kind of reasoning from mechanical principles; for I am induced by many reasons to suspect that they all depend upon certain forces by which the particles of bodies by some causes hitherto unknown, are either mutually impelled towards each other and cohere in regular figures, or are repelled and recede from each other; which forces being unknown, philosophers have hitherto attempted the search of

> nature in vain. But I hope the principles here laid down will afford some light either to that or some true method of philosophy. (Taylor 1962: 143-44)

Not that the scientists themselves are totally unaware of misrepresentation through style. P.W. Bridgman, for one, emphasizes the role of the individual in scientific research and advocates a first person report as well as the use of such 'introspectional' words as 'think', 'feel', 'conscious', where necessary (Bridgman 1959). I have discussed the implications of Bridgman's ideas on technical expression in a separate paper (Sharma 1981: 207-17). The use of the specific forms of language will, of course, depend on the nature of the science or experiment concerned.

The main point is that the conventions of style must not be allowed to misrepresent the true nature of the reality being described. In some cases, the proof may be so conclusive that any use of introspectional words will be ridiculous. In other cases, not only introspectional words but even many kinds of limiting and qualifying expressions will be needed, e.g. "How the drug will affect the human organism after prolonged use, or the foetus in pregnant woman is still not known."

It is particularly important today to warn against the misuse of technical style. Things and drugs are produced and consumed at a mass-scale, and the overriding consideration of the producer is quick profit. The big companies and multinationals maintain their own research facilities where thousands of research workers earn their livelihood. Under these circumstances, there exists a powerful inducement for the scientist to develop a bias in favour of his employer, for he who pays the piper should call the tune.

Glottopolitics

The term 'glottopolitics' is not very common in the literature. It deals with the problems which involve language matters at the level of political decisions and governmental policy (Hall 1964: 461). However, the topics associated with this branch of study have often been assimilated to socio-linguistics. I wish to revive the term in a new sense to which, in my view, it is more appropriate, namely, tongue politics or language politics: politics done with the deployment of language as a weapon.

The term 'politics' itself denotes two kinds of activities. Accordingly, I shall divide it into 'high politics' and 'low politics'. High politics is the art or science of power and government on the basis of political documents, formal declarations on behalf of states, international agreements, etc. It is characterized by seriousness of purpose, sincerity, concern for the welfare of the people, and certain political norms. The language of high politics is outside the scope of this paper, but we must keep it in mind to serve as a norm.

Our chief concern here is with low politics, which may be defined as "the scheming and manoeuvring for power and personal advantage" (Reader's Digest, *Great Illustrated Dictionary*). But first we must notice a general characteristic. Hayakawa has observed a two-valued orientation in politics. For a Republican, whatever his party does is good and whatever the Democrats do is bad. Hayakawa, feels, however, that in a two-party system, it is not always possible to maintain a two-valued orientation, since the parties have to cooperate on many occasions. But when a single party holds sway as in Hitler's Germany, the two-valued orientation is very clear. The Nazis declared that whoever was the enemy of the National Socialist Party, was an enemy of Germany (1952: 231-32). The two-valued system sees things as *white* and *black*, or *white* and *non-white* and this is clearly reflected in the vocabulary of politics. We should notice that such a division of reality is fallacious; it is an absurd simplification of the facts of life. Still, we have to admit that this is how things have been going on for centuries; perhaps the human mind has not yet become refined enough to operate with the multi-valued system.

However that may be, the two-valued orientation has been extended to the international sphere with the emergence of two opposing camps dominated by the superpowers respectively. You have to look at the political scene either through the American or the Soviet lenses. This state of affairs has given rise to an interesting stylistic feature of the vocabulary of politics, particularly low politics. Words are charged with strong connotation as favourable or unfavourable and are hurled as weapons: 'democracy'/'Communism', 'bourgeois'/ 'communist'; 'free enterprise'/'state ownership'; 'reactionary'/ 'progressive'; 'terrorist'/'revolutionary'; 'traitor'/'patriot', and so on. The situation becomes laughable when antonymic expressions are applied to the same referent: Gaddafi is a terrorist for Reagan, but a revolutionary for Russia, the present rulers of Afghanistan and Nicaragua are lawful governments of those countries, in the eyes of Russia, but they are usurpers according to the U.S.

Each nation has its sovereignty and this sovereignty is implicitly extended to the use of words: the rulers of the world have a right to use the language the way they like, irrespective of its appropriateness and meaning. This kind of licence is possible only because, in terms of reality, might is still right in the international arena. President Reagan has, for example, declared that he ordered air strikes against Libya in "self-defence" because Gaddafi was running "terrorist" centres in his country. At one stroke the U.S. President has widened the meaning of "self-defence" beyond the modest calculations of the lexicographer. But we should not forget that this is a weapon used, an artifice, and no longer a word out of the dictionary, for, if India were to attack Pakistan tomorrow on the same ground, the word Mr. Reagan will most probably deploy is its opposite, 'aggression'. Chase has quoted a striking example of a word used for cheating: "In 1920, a presidential candidate in the United States election told a reporter that, "Americanism was to be this year's campaign issue". When the newspaperman asked him what 'Americanism' meant, he said that "he did not know, but that it was a damned good word with which to carry out an election" (1938: 241). I guess such 'damned good words' keep turning up in every election everywhere.

This leads up to the second characteristic of the political style: use of vague and non-informative language. This takes several forms: very general and polymeric or ambiguous words, counter-questions, abstractions, repetitions. Take up any reported interview with a politician and you will find a language which refuses to reward the reader with much new specific information and which avoids commitment. I have heard a saying that if a politician says 'yes' it means 'may be' if he says 'may be' it means 'no' and if he says 'no' he is not a politician.

A constant problem before a politician is to make his present position agree with his past utterances, for, we must know, a politician is never wrong. You seldom find a Gandhi who can admit having committed a Himalayan blunder. How does this happen? Well, the inconsistency is removed by a jugglery of words. We shall analyse one example. A few days before the U.S. attack on Libya, Mrs. Thatcher was reported to have said that Britain would not allow the use of F-111 planes stationed in the country in an *attack against Libya* (*The Hindustan Times,* April 14, 1986). When the attack did take place, she explained that she had always been in favour of hitting the *terrorist centres in Libya.* We can see how a distinction is made between 'attacking Libya' and 'attacking the terrorist centres in Libya'. In the meantime the deception has worked. She also strengthened her contention by saying that the F-111's were capable "of precise surgical operation" (*The Times of India,* April 16, 1986).

Politicians make use of three kinds of style along the interpersonal dimension, each of which is liable to misuse. I shall call these, style of identity, style of integration, and style of distance. Each style has its own meaning. In the first, the leader identifies himself with the nation and speaks on behalf of it; in the second he presents himself as a part of the people, and in the third, he separates himself from the people. These styles are based on the political realities of a society and their use is valid as long as they truthfully represent these realities. These styles are achieved chiefly by the choice of appropriate pronouns and noun phrases and they may be used singly or may be mixed to produce a variety of effects. Let us examine some portions of Ronald Reagan's carefully constructed address of 1986 to the joint session of U.S. Congress.

Reagan makes a threefold distinction: himself, Congress, the people or nation. This is quite understandable for he has to highlight his personal initiative, he must recognise Congress as a political entity and he must speak of the people as distinct from government; he must also integrate himself with one or the other, or both as the exigencies of psychological rapport demand. Let us consider the following sentences:

1. I have come to review with you the progress of our nation.
2. Tonight the American people deserve our thanks.
3. Despite the pressure of our modern world, family and community remain the moral core of our society. (SPAN, March, 1986: 42).

In the first sentence, the President and the Congress are at the outset quite distinct, but he hastens to weld them into one, 'our nation'. In the second, he conceives a distinction between himself and the Congress, on the one hand, and the American people on the other. In the third ("our society") he rolls all the three into a single unit. (Note that 'our' has a different connotation in "our modern world".)

The style of his speech is perfectly genuine. But imagine Zia-ul-Haq identifying himself with the nation, saying, for example, that Pakistan will not hold elections until 1990. This is artifice, for according to modern democratic norms he cannot do so; he is simply misleading the hearer. On the other hand, if he says, "I will not hold elections until 1990" he is using the style of distance to assert his power over the people. If he says, "We will not hold the elections until 1990", he is without proper content integrating himself with the people and implicating them in what is virtually his own decision. All the three utterances, therefore, are in the final analysis, deceitful because they do not represent the proper content.

Advertising

The language of press advertising shows many characteristics which properly belong to literature. But when it is subjected to rigorous analysis, the similarities turn out to be merely superficial and the underlying motive not commendable

(Quirk 1962: 252). First let us enumerate the stylistic devices used in the language of advertising. Looking at the vocabulary, we find new compounds, coinages, and words with a new spelling; particularly advertisers are fond of coining new adjective compounds (Leech 1974: 37). There is also a good deal of rhetoric. Naryanaswami has noted word play as an important device in the English used in Indian advertising (CIEFL 1980: 203). We have examples of simile, metaphor, pun and some other figures of speech. The syntax has its own distinctive aspects (Leech 1966). Structure words are sparingly used. Phrases and even single words are made to serve as statements. Interrogatives and imperatives are liberally used. Semantically, the vocabulary is expressive, directive. Connotative items, mostly favourable, are quite common.

The description of the language of advertising, however, tells us very little about its stylistic content. We must probe deeper in order to discover its true intent and meanings. We shall take some examples, but first we must note that modern advertising is a composite affair: the language of an advertisement generally accompanies some picture and has to be considered in relation to that picture.

There is a picture of Onida, with a broken screen, and above it, the following text:

> The most envied colour TV
> Within a stone's throw!
> Now who'd want to hurl a
> stone at such a beautiful TV;
> Mentally, though, many might,
> Some of your neighbours for
> instance. Who may have seen
> your new ONIDA, And envied
> its colour, futuristic look, the
> most astounding true-to-life
> colour, and the sharpest picture
> They 'ave ever seen on a TV
> screen! And have been deeply
> regretting the fact that they're
> stuck with colour TVs that are

obviously a generation behind!
You may of course argue, your
neighbours are the nicest lot,
Hardly the type to stoop to
Violence no matter how much
They envy your ONIDA TV.
Well, thank heavens!

The caption is as usual a phrase with structure words kept to a minimum; it attacks the reader's mind, with a concrete image: 'stone's throw' is a hackneyed expression, but it produces a solid effect; moreover in the next sentence, it is further utilised in a word-play. The statement is placed on an emotional plane by using the mark of exclamation. The highly connotative word 'envied' is used with the superlative—the use of superlative is very common in advertising. The other examples in this text are "most astounding", "sharpest", "nicest". There is an assumption that Onida is the most envied colour TV, forcibly, as it were, imposed on the reader. Throughout the text it is taken for granted that whatever is said about the product is true and this amounts to a kind of psychological deception. The epithets used for Onida are from the smart language of the fashionable: "classy", "beautiful", "futuristic", "true-to-life".

The next sentence, again is an exclamation, made striking by its interrogative form. The note of exclamation intensifies the rhetorical question. You are made to feel with excitement that no one would like to damage the set. On a closer study we discover that the devious connection with "stone's throw" is no more than a trick; it has no real logic, it is childish word-play. The next line is elliptical; it also has alliteration but without significance—as a student of literature would know. The theme of envy continues in the second section. The first sentence is highly elliptical. In fact, what should be part of a sentence is broken up into several fragments, each written as an independent sentence with a mark of exclamation. The good qualities of Onida are 'crisply' set out and an unfavourable expression is used for the other TVs: "Obviously a generation behind". We then get one sentence written as two sentences, containing the highly emotive unfavourable term "violence". These two sentences are statements. Then comes the last, which is an exclamation. The whole matter has been divided into what appear to be stanzas of a poem.

We soon discover that the mechanical form of the text is far from poetry or any profound thought; that it is as deceptively clothed as an ordinary message into a poetic form. You feel cheated by too many exclamations which fail to raise your emotions. The form does not have a corresponding content. We also become aware of another trick. It is assumed that the reader has recently bought an Onida: "Who may have seen your new Onida." The device is used to put the reader in a state of dream—a dream of how it feels to own an Onida, described from the neighbours' point of view. From the informative point of view, the passage has nothing new to offer. It proceeds from the assumption that Onida is the best TV, and then it assails your feelings. That is why Hayakawa has labelled advertisements as anti-information (1952: 291). There is a great deal of tautological deception in advertisements and trade-inscriptions. A product for example may be described as "rich in vitamins and minerals", which in fact tells nothing new: it simply says that vitamin and minerals naturally occur in that product.

There is, however, enough, in the language of advertisement to beguile the common reader and consumer, for often he does not understand the subtle mechanism of deceptive and emotional exploitation which is employed. We must, therefore, explore further the basic ways of advertising.

First, the object of advertising, is to make you desire the thing. It focuses on our hopes, fears and dreams, including romance. The images of these states are flowers, beautiful women, handsome young couples, smiling child, mother with child, and comfortable home. The negative images of diseased body, old men and women, worried posture are also utilised. We may also add film-stars, sportsmen, 21st century, and spacecraft to the appealing images. These are the recurring motifs. Next, these images are often arbitrarily associated with the product, otherwise; as a psychologist has observed, what have bikini-clad lovelies to do with a bulldozer.

So the picture is there to put you in a good mood, or if a negative one, to make you receptive to the message. Then follows the text, which may or may not refer to the picture, but the picture is an important element of the context. As we have seen, the style is intended to make an emotional appeal and not to give facts about the product, although it may foreground what it says are the good features. Statements about the product are presented as already confirmed and imperatives are used to exhort the reader to buy the product. An important device in most advertisements is to relate the product to the reader through the images I have mentioned, by means of the pronoun 'you'. This will be clear from some more examples.

An advertisement for Amul Chocolates contains the picture of a bunch of flowers with different Amul Chocolate packets attached to flowers. It says: "A gift for someone you love." Another advertisement presents mother and' child and the text: "Great warm moments. Created by your love and Vardhmann knitting yarn." An insurance advertisement presents a couple with the child in the man's arms and advises: "Live without fear." Another tactic is to hold up some one or something as a symbol of good or standard living. "He has his teeth insured", "His TVS 50 XL makes him feel free as a bird"; "For homes that stay beautiful...look what it's done to him." There are also variations with the first person pronoun or just epigrammatic description: "I was only an occasional coffee drinker, until I tasted Bru Instant"; "A royal view, and a suiting to match"; "On my lips, cherries smile, In my heart I'm feeling good!" "For some people, choosing the best is a way of life."

The language of advertisement is very carefully chosen: its words and constructions appeal, surprise at every turn, and subtly exploit your emotions. That is why the text of an advertisement when it has become quite familiar needs change. But the stylistic devices do not change: we still have connotative vocabulary, arbitrary association, word-play, exclamations, imperatives, and calculated use of pronouns.

Muddling

By 'Muddling' I mean using language as an expedient in order to cover up lack of knowledge or clear understanding or to make an ordinary fact or principle appear complex and profound. We all face such problems at time in the course of exposition of some subject and even in conversation. The alternatives are either to make a modest admission and state the plain fact plainly or to resort to artifice and deceive the reader or hearer. I think if we pay careful attention to others' conversation and exposition, we can detect spots where the style becomes turbid, as it were, by comparison with the general tenor of the discourse. For example, in the course of a conversation, a person may find himself at a juncture when he has to hide something. On such an occasion he will resort to an abstract style, periphrastic expression, or he may go pseudo-technical. This brief change will not be a matter of vocabulary alone, it will affect syntax and tone as well, and may involve the use of some formulaic expressions designed to face such difficulties. I take the first example from *Lucky Jim,* a novel by Kingsley Amis. Michie has just asked Dixon to give him some idea of the new course the latter was going to teach.

> 'Well, I think the main emphasis of the thing will be social, you know.' He was trying to stop himself from thinking directly about the official title of his subject, which was 'Medieval Life and Culture'. 'I thought I might start with a discussion of the university, for instance, in its social role'. He comforted himself for having said this by the thought that at least he knew it didn't mean anything. (28)

Degnan, in an article included in Reader's Digest book, *Word Power,* has cited an interesting example of clothing a simple idea in a bafflingly learned style:

> The choice of exogenous variables in relation to multicolinearity is contingent upon the derivations of certain multiple correlation coefficients.

The author tells us that all that the student, who wrote this, wanted to say was "supply determines demand" (1980: 121). Degnan is, however, less than fair to Chomsky and

Harris, when he includes them among his "masters of babble" (22). On the other hand, he is perfectly right in diagnosing the cause of the malady (123). Like impersonal style, what may be called learned style has established its tyranny to such an extent that many who wish to survive in the intellectual sphere are forced to use artifice in their linguistic expression.

Fallacies

The discussion of fallacies covers a vast area. Fischer (1971), has described more than one hundred different types of fallacies. Copi (1978) presents a simple and selective treatment of both formal and informal fallacies. My aim is not to discuss fallacies from a purely logical point of view, nor to present an exhaustive view. I wish to consider fallacies as linguistic strategies employed to gain undue advantage or the upper hand. However, it must be realised that in a linguistic analysis involving semantics, logical criteria cannot be dispensed with altogether.

We begin by proposing a principle, which, I must admit is tentative and cannot probably account for all kinds of fallacies: a fallacy involves confusion of two semantic fields in an argument, clearly set out or implied. By 'Semantic field' I simply mean a lexical complex, representing one particular area of human experience. As pointed out by Lyons, the terminology used in this part of semantic study is variable and uncertain (1977: 250-51); nevertheless, the terms I am using, will I hope become clear in the course of practical analysis which follows. I must add that the lexical items within a field are held together by certain kinds of semantic relations and, what is more important in our context, each item has a value. Thus the framework proposed here places at our disposal certain definite tools of analysis at the linguistic level. In studying the text of a fallacy, we have to recognise two semantic fields and to identify the key terms which are employed to confuse the logic of an argument. Sometimes an accompanying syntactic shift is also present and calls for a syntactic analysis as well.

We shall begin with an example cited by Copi. At the "Big Three" meeting at Yalta, "Churchill is reported to have told the others that the Pope had suggested that such and such a course of action would be right. And Stalin is said to have indicated his disagreement by asking "And how many divisions did you say the Pope had available for combat duty?" (88-89).

Technically, the fallacy committed in Stalin's rejoinder is called *argumentum ad baculum* (appeal to force). According to our procedure, the key-term is 'division', which has its place as well as value in a semantic field: it indicates military force. On the other hand, the keyword in Churchill's statement is 'the Pope', which, again, represents a value in another field. The fallacy is created by Stalin's use of a discordant semantic field in the frame of the argument. We should also notice the syntax. Stalin's rejoinder is couched in the interrogative form preceded by 'and', which is more than a connective in this pattern—compare, for example, 'and what will happen if I don't'. The question of course is rhetorical. The form of the sentence is intended to strengthen the argument. In this case the fallacious utterance is marked off from the rest by a syntactic shift.

The example, we are considering, needs further analysis, for Churchill's own contention is also fallacious. The area of discourse is international diplomacy and we expect the arguments to remain on the plane of the relevant semantic fields. Churchill, however, seeks to justify a certain course of action on the ground that the Pope considered it right by using a high-value ecclesiastical term to distort the logic.

Another common fallacy is called *argumentum ad hominem* in which unfavourable expressions are applied to some person in order to support the conclusion. Numerous examples of this kind of fallacy can be found in literary criticism. Take the following statement by F.R. Leavis:

> The opposition to the Georgians was already at the time in question (just after the war) Sitwellism. But the Sitwells belong to the history of publicity rather than of poetry. (1932: 64)

The word 'publicity' stands out as a discordant element. It shares a semantic field with 'propaganda', 'advertising', and some other terms. The word has an unfavourable connotation, and strictly speaking it does not belong to the area of literary experience. Thus, Leavis dismisses the work of the Sitwells by abusing them. The syntax and some stylistic features, e.g. alliteration and the mode of conjoining 'publicity' and 'poetry', are also noticeable.

I have tried to explain two kinds of fallacies by a single linguistic principle. We can extend its application to many other informal fallacies by making a deeper analysis. I shall mention here three more fallacies which I have particularly noticed and which are stylistically interesting.

The first may be called the fallacy of objective-attitude. It is characterized by distinctive syntactic structure and vocabulary. The utterance opens with a sentence adverbial containing as an important constituent an objectivity-word: 'objectively speaking', 'to be fair and impartial', 'if we take a dispassionate view'. The fallacy arises from the fact that the speaker wants us to assume that, since he has used such adverbials, he is in fact impartial. If this were so, such adverbials would be a characteristic feature of scientific style, which is not the case.

The second type may be called the fallacy of authority. The language is characterized by the naming of an authority and by quotation. The argument will be fallacious only where the conclusion is wrongly asserted solely on the basis of an authority, and not in all cases. If I were to conclude that Hamlet is a defective play on the ground that T.S. Eliot says so, I shall be guilty of committing this fallacy: if, on the other hand, I draw this conclusion logically from a consideration of the play itself, there will be no fallacy, although the whole argument may be challenged. We are also aware of the misuse of authority in deciding questions of grammar and usage. The fallacy is compounded, as it were, when the authority mentioned is not an expert on the subject of the argument. In advertising, a product is said to be the best because a great film-star or cricketer says so. A related fallacy is the fallacy of partial quotation, where only the favourable part of an original statement by an authority is quoted in support of a conclusion. This fallacy had led to many misinterpretations. A well-known case in literary circles is the partial quotation of Wordsworth's definition of poetry: "Poetry is the spontaneous overflow of powerful feelings." There is also an important group of fallacies all of which are grounded on some kind of ambiguity. They will lead themselves easily to linguistic analysis—including phonological. It can also be shown that these fallacies are amenable to the method of analysis I have suggested.

Formal fallacies are more a matter of logic than of language. It is possible to describe the language of formal fallacies, but the task, I think is difficult and may not be very fruitful from the linguistic point of view.

Journalese

The language of journalism has already been commented on by linguists (Crystal and Davy 1969: 173-92; Turner 1973: 123-24; Leech 1974: 40-41). We must, however, distinguish between the language of newspaper reporting and journalese: the former is a genuine and useful activity concerned to disseminate new information, but may often degenerate into the latter, which seeks to overpower the reader's mind by false surprise and sensationalism. It is thus not newspaper reporting as such but journalese which constitutes artifice, and the term with its pejorative connotation is particularly appropriate to the present study.

Journalism makes use of a kind of jargon which results in a crude simplification and sensationalisation of a complex reality. The headlines are packed with strongly dynamic and connotative words and are condensed to the extent of misleading ambiguity. Take the following examples chosen at random: "5 labourers buried alive"; "6th Fleet bares its fangs"; "Zia spurns Benazir plea for early poll"; "More to sharpen defence teeth"; "US judge flays lawyers' conduct". The first of these reports an accident in which five labourers were killed. The syntactic ambiguity may, however, lead to a serious misinterpretation. The other headlines also distort the news-content by semantical intensification; for example, 'spurn' is used to report Zia-ul-Haq's statement that Benazir should wait till 1990 for the election, and the U.S. Judge's critical remarks are 'heightened' through the metaphor of flaying. When we remember that hundreds of news-items are read by many people only in the headlines, we can imagine how much damage is being caused by misuse of language in journalese. We shall consider one example in more detail.

Vajpayee for Army Control

> The BJP leader, Mr. Atal Behari Vajpayee, today suggested that military should be called in Punjab to control the worsening law and order situation. Addressing a public meeting here yesterday, Mr. Vajpayee said that drastic action should be taken against the extremists, and anti-social elements creating disturbances in Punjab.
>
> He said Punjab Chief Minister, Surjit Singh Barnala should seek military assistance.
>
> (*The Hindustan Times*, April 11, 1986: 5)

We notice that the headline is ambiguous at two levels: the verbless clause is not clear in meaning, specially because the preposition 'for' is capable of various interpretations, and the phrase 'army control' has a stronger meaning, which is not intended here. Shorn of the qualifier which could limit and localise it, this noun phrase turns the too-familiar attitude of Vajpayee into an astonishing declaration. The specific meaning conveyed in para 1, however, explains the deception and we perceive the improper equating of 'help of the army' with 'army control'. Similarly, at the end, Barnala is advised to seek 'military assistance', which in normal usage denotes help of a different kind and magnitude by a foreign power. The rest of the passage is full of hackneyed journalistic expressions. The result of the style is that it presents as news something which has little that is new.

Our analysis has hinted at the central problem of journalism: that of manufacturing news out of much that is familiar or probable. Since the situation does not change as often as the daily editions of newspapers—the position of party leaders remains the same meeting after meeting and their exhortations are mostly repetitions—the newspapermen resort to stylistic devices in order to capture the public mind: where reality does not show appreciable alteration, it must be distorted through journalese.

Concluding Remarks

Choice of language to suit a situation or to serve the speaker's purpose is of greater practical consequence than conformity to grammar. This is not to say that the latter does not count in language-use; it is indeed the foundation on which stylistic variation can be based. Nevertheless, grammaticalness is mostly unconscious and is usually taken for granted. Grammatical errors, where they occur, are easily assigned to carelessness or lack of mastery of the language system, and we do not attempt to see an intention behind them; they have no more practical consequence except where the error is so serious that it causes ambiguity or misinterpretation. When I decide to use a third person singular, almost automatically I combine it with the appropriate form of the verb, and if somehow I don't, redundancy in the system and the 'understanding' of the hearer make up for the deficiency—no harm is done.

On the other hand, when I decide to employ the passive sentence instead of the active, or an imperative instead of a modal utterance, I am making a calculated move in order to produce a certain effect or influence the situation in a certain way. Therefore, linguistic choices embodied in a style deserve our serious consideration if we are viewing language as a social tool which must be used properly, but which may also be misused for personal advantage.

In the present article, I have considered employment of style as a stratagem to cheat, mislead, and dominate others. This involves value-judgements, and the question is whether value-judgements have any place in a scientific study. To settle this issue, we must take account of two things. First, as we have already seen, it is erroneous to believe that the scientist is totally free from value-judgements. There are many subtle ways in which scientific research is influenced by at least a general conception of what is good and what is bad. Moreover, whenever scientific results are considered in the context of human life, value-judgements are bound to be present in the background. When a scientist explains how nuclear fusion takes place and how much energy is released, value-judgement is negligible, but when he tells what diseases may be caused by excessive radiation, or how many human beings can be killed by a hydrogen bomb, value-judgements are certainly involved.

Secondly, the nature of the value-judgements implicit in the present investigation must be clearly perceived. I have provided a descriptive touchstone for the proper and improper use of style. It will be remembered that I have taken an integral view of style: style represents a certain kind of content, it symbolizes an aspect of reality. If on analysis we find that the style of a text does not have the appropriate content or aspect of reality, we conclude that the style may have been misused. When this conclusion is borne out by the context, we become confirmed in our opinion. Thus value-judgements involved in this paper are based on factual and analytical criteria and not on impressions or arbitrary personal decisions.

That there is need for investigations along these lines will, I hope, be conceded. It is s a matter of common experience that in this age of propaganda, political jobbery, and economic exploitation, language is being used daily for what must be called unethical ends. Language-use has to be considered in the context of social health and illness. It is, therefore, in order that I should conclude by Korzybski's words from his "Foreword" to Dr. Lee's book:

> The future thus depends upon our ability to discover and use the methods of sanity in speech and action. Distorted neurolinguistic performances by present-day abnormal "Fuhrers" have already affected the linguistic habits of politicians, etc., who knew how to abuse language before, but not to such a pathological extent. Already endless harm has been done to the public and military morale, and special measures will have to be taken to prevent the contagious disease of the pathological use of language from being perpetuated indefinitely. (Lee 1941: x)

Works Cited

Akhmanova, Olga 1976. *Linguostylisitics: Theory and Method.* The Hague: Mouton.

Babb, H.S. (ed.) 1972. *Essays in Stylistic Analysis,* New York: Harcourt Brace Jovanovich Inc.

Beveridge, W.I.B. 1950. *The Art of Scientific Investigation,* Rev. ed. New York: Random House, 1957.

Bloch, B. 1953. "Linguistic Structure and Linguistic Analysis". In: *Report of the Fourth Annual Round Table Meeting on Linguistics and Language Teaching.* Washington D.C. 1953.

Bridgman, P.W. 1959. *The Way Things Are.* Harvard University Press.

Chase, S. 1938. *The Tyranny of Words.* 3rd ed. London: Math.

Conant, J.B. 1952. *Modern Science and Modern Man.* New York: Columbia University Press.

Copi, I.M. 1953. *Introduction to Logic.* 5th ed. New York: Macmillan, 1978.

Crystal, D. and Davy, D. 1969. *Investigating English Style.* London: Longman.

Degnan, J.P. 1976. "Masters of Babble". In: Reader's Digest, *Word Power,* 1980.

Epstein, E.L. 1978. *Language and Style.* London: Methuen.

Fischer, D.H. 1978. *Historians' Fallacies.* London: Routledge and Kegan Paul.

Hall, R.A. 1964. *Introductory Linguistics.* Indian ed. Delhi: Motilal Banarasidass, 1969.

Halliday, M.A.K., McIntosh, A., and Strevens, P. 1964. *The Linguistic Sciences and Language Teaching.* London: ELBS.

Hayakawa, S.I. 1952. *Language in Thought and Action.* 2nd ed. London: George Allen and Unwin, 1965.

Hintikka, J. 1976. *Language Games,* In: Saarinen (1979: 1-26).

Kelly, R.A. 1962. *The Use of English for Technical Students.* London : ELBS.

Korzybski, A. 1921. *Manhood of Humanity: The Science and Art of Human Engineering.* New York: E.P. Dutton.

——. 1933. *Science and Sanity.* 2nd ed. 3rd large printing. Lakeville: The International Non-Aristotelian Library Publishing Co., 1950.

——. 1941. "Foreword". In Lee (1941).

Leavis, F.R. 1932. *New Bearings in English Poetry.* Peregrine Books. Harmondsworth: Penguin, 1963.

Lee, Irving J. 1941. *Language Habits in Human Affairs.* New York: Harper and Brothers Publishers.

Leech, G.N. 1966. *English in Advertising: A Linguistic Study of Advertising in Great Britain.* London: Longman.

Leech, G.N. 1974. *Semantics,* Harmondsworth: Penguin.

Leech, G.N. and Short, M.H. 1981. *Style in Fiction: A Linguistic Introduction to English Fictional Prose.* London: Longman.

Lenz, W. 1962. "Thalidomide and Congenital Abnormalities". *Lancet,* 1:45.

Lyons, J. 1977. *Semantics-I.* London: Cambridge University Press.

——. 1981. *Language and Linguistics.* London: Cambridge Univ. Press.

McBride, W.G. 1961. "Thalidomide and Congenital Abnormalities". *Lancet,* 2: 1358.

Narayanswami, V.R. 1980. "English in Indian advertising". In CIEFL, *Issues in Stylistics.* Hyderabad: CIEFL.

Ohmann, R.M. 1959. "Prolegomena to the Analysis of Prose Style". In: Babb (1972: 36-49).

Quirk, R. 1962. *The Use of English.* 2nd ed. London: ELBS, 1972.

Saarinen, E.S.A. (ed.) 1979. *Game—theoretical Semantics.* Dordrecht: D. Reidel Publishing Company.

Sharma, R.S. 1975. "Teaching Materials in Technical English". *Indian Journal of Applied Linguistics* (1.2).

——. 1978. "The Teaching of Technical English in the Indian Context". *IRAL,* XVI/2.

——. 1981. "Technical Style: Implications of Operationalism". *IDELTI Journal* (18) (Baghdad).

——. 1982a. *Linguistic Aspects of Contemporary English Poetry.* Varanasi: Academic Publishers.

——. 1983b. "Teaching Semantic Distinction through Literature". *IRAL,* XXIII/3.

——. 1985c. *Technical Writing.* Varanasi: Academic Publishers.

Somers, G.F. 1960. Pharmacological properties of thalidomide and phthalimido Glutarimide): A new sedative hypnotic drug. *British Journal of Pharmocology and Chemotherapy* (15).

Taylor, F.S. 1943. *Science Past and Present.* London: Mercury Books, 1962.

Turner, G.W. 1973. *Stylistics.* Harmondsworth: Penguin.

Wittgenstein, L. 1953. *Philosophical Investigations.* Tr. G.E.M. Anscombe, 3rd ed. Oxford: Basil Blackwell, 1967.

Zamyatin, 1972. *We.* Tr. B.G. Guerney. Harmondsworth: Penguin.

Meaning and Grammar in Poetry

'Meaning' is a difficult concept and its scope has gone on expanding as a result of modern researches. "The word 'meaning' and its corresponding verb 'to mean' are among the most eminently discussable terms in the English language and semanticists have often seemed to spend an immoderate amount of time puzzling out the 'meaning of meaning' as a supposedly necessary preliminary to the study of their subject" (Leech 1981: 1). When we embark upon a study of meaning in poetry in a practical context, the problem grows in magnitude and complexity and some kind of theory of poetic use of words becomes indispensable. One simple solution is offered by I.A. Richards, who has outlined two uses of language. "A statement may be used for the sake of the reference, true or false, which it causes. This is the scientific use of language. But it may also be used for the sake of the effects in emotion and attitude produced by the reference it occasions. This is the emotive use of language" (1924: 211). Poetry makes an emotive use of language. It involves conversion of reference and denotation into connotation. This does not mean that reference and denotation have no role to play in poetic discourse. In fact, rational and ideational content in a poem forms the foundation on which the aesthetic experience is grounded. It would be wrong to assume that the reference to Milton, the poet, and England has nothing to do with the meaning and effect of the following lines:

Milton thou shouldst be living at this hour:
England hath need of thee: she is a fen
of stagnant water: altar, sword, and pen
Fireside, the heroic wealth of hall and bower,
Have forfeited their ancient English dower
of inward happiness.

True, the final feeling of lack of 'manners, virtue, freedom, power' in Wordsworth's England and of the need of a poet of Milton's stature is the experience to be gained from the poem, yet the experience itself is inextricably linked with reference. "The rational structure underlying a poem is like the skeleton underneath the flesh, the rose of the cheek and the velvet of the breast: it is like the bough on which the blossom sits; it is the thought on which the feeling flowers" (Sharma 1985: 40).

Thus, poetry is not simply a matter of using connotative words, it involves exploiting every type of meaning with such art that the resultant effect is of an emotive nature. Nor is this process confined to words alone; it actually encompasses all levels of languages as well as artistic form. Susanne K. Langer in her book, *Feeling and Form*, has developed a theory of art according to which all artistic form is an indirect expression of feeling (1953). We can therefore say that the meaning of a poem is in the feeling it embodies and the feeling is in the form. Form we must insist, includes the linguistic form comprising not only sound and words, but also morphology and syntax i.e. grammar. Now this is a fact which the literary critic often ignores while dealing with poetic form; his concept of form is confined to such things as image, symbol, rhythm, rhyme, stanza.

Our endeavour in the present paper will be to demonstrate the meaning of grammar, that is, the grammatical meaning in poetry. As a preliminary, we shall cast a close look at the concept of meaning, particularly its scope. Leech has identified seven types of meaning; these are: conceptual, connotative, social, affective, reflected, collocative, thematic. This, as admitted by the author, cannot be taken as a complete catalogue, nor is the demarcation, between one type of meaning and another always easy to make (1981: 9-23).

On the empirical plane, if the total response to a word or sentence is treated as its meaning, then meaning, has a very wide scope and will include, percept, concept, idea, feeling, relation, attitude and a lot more. The distinction between content and structure words will break down at a deeper level and it will be observed that even prepositions and modals are meaningful. Variation and repetition of grammatical structure are also not without meaning in the broad sense we have adopted. A broad view of meaning is necessary when it comes to analyzing and interpreting poetry, because in poetry, what is considered marginal in common discourse, is of utmost importance—attitude, feeling, tone.

In poetic language, like meaning, grammar too has a wider scope than is generally accepted. In addition to the normal patterns and their variation, we have to take into account deviation of various kinds and even lack of grammar.

We shall now proceed to illustrate the above categories and we begin with the last, namely, lack of grammar or zero grammar. Grammar binds our mental images, impressions and concepts into a rational structure: one of its major functions is relational meaning. Therefore words divested of a grammatical structure will present to us the most raw experience which has a beauty and vividness of its own. There has been in modern poetry a deliberate attempt to acquire freedom, to varying degrees, from the tyranny of grammar. The movement can be traced back to Rimbaud who "disposed not merely with grammar and syntax when necessary and with the dictionary meaning of words, writing his most mature poetry in 'prose'; he stripped away in so doing all connecting links that stood in the way of the essential vision" (Rodman 1951: X). Whole poems completely devoid of grammar are not often met with, but zero grammar and partial grammar are often employed for special effects.

मैं अकेला;
देखता हूँ, आ रही
मेरे दिवस की सांध्य बेला।

(Nirala)

Most linguists would treat the first line as a minor sentence with the deep structure form.

मैं अकेला हूँ।

But this rational imposition will work against the precise effect intended. In epistemological terms also the cupola in such sentence is a linguistic construct used to convert the experience into a sentence; it is illusory. In some language, such as Arabic, it is not used at all. So the poet has done away with this misleading item. The semi-colon at the end of the line marks it off as an independent unit. The line, therefore, presents the poet as a lonely being, detached from his own reality and looking at it as an observer. The following poem by Charles Madge also presents experience quintessentially with reduced grammar:

Scene

A Coloured page, a coloured piece of glass
A reverie, a picture of a man
An element, a wand, a wandering mind

Here we have an assemblage of noun phrases denoting perceptual and conceptual images producing a static effect; the absence of verbs excludes any kinaesthetic experience, and lack of connecting items prevents any temporal and spatial perspective from emerging apart from the succession of the phrases in print. The experience presented is suspended in the air, as it were.

There is another noticeable feature in these lines: a repeated use of the indefinite Article *a*. In terms of the modulation of feeling, this grammatical patterning is very meaningful. It emphasizes the indefiniteness of the perception aroused by the scene. The experience rises in the mind like a vision which cannot be definitely related to history or to any place.

This is an example of a normal pattern 'Overused'. The feature is called 'deviance' which may be defined as "purely statistical notion: as the difference between the normal frequency of a feature and its frequency in the text or corpus"

(Leech and Short 1981: 48). Another example of deviance is to be seen in the following lines by Phillip Larkin:

> The bottle is drunk out by one;
> At two, the book is shut;
> At three the lovers lie apart,
> Love and its commerce done;

Out of the four verbs used in this passage, three are in the passive voice, and the passive clauses are without the agentive phrase. This high frequency of the agentiveless passive is bound to engage our attention. The passive without the agentive phrase is a stylistic feature of the register of science and technology; it is associated with impersonality, objectivity and mechanicalness:

> One of the first methods of making steel was invented in England in 1856 by Sir Henry Bessemer. In the Bessemer process, about 25 ton of molten pig iron is poured into a huge egg-shaped converter that has a perforated bottom through which compressed air is blown. As the blast of hot air bubbles through the molten iron, the carbon is oxidised to carbon dioxide and escapes.
>
> (Keenan and Wood, General College Chemistry)

When we compare this passage with the lines of poetry under study we become aware in the latter of a clear discord between matter and manner. The semantic content of the piece is concerned with the subjective experience of pleasures: drinking, reading, making love. It requires lyrical syntax first person singular, active voice, modifiers, exclamations, as in,

> My heart leaps up when I behold
> A rainbow in the sky
>
> (Wordsworth)

> O my Luve's Like a red, red rose
> That's newly sprung in June:
> O my Luve's like the melodie
> That's sweetly play'd in tune.
>
> (Burns)

This discrepancy between content and form is the chief source of the ironical meaning these lines transmit; the lyrical content is poured into an impersonal mould with the result that we are made to realise how the activities of personal joy and satisfaction are performed by the modern man mechanically like meaningless rituals. Incidentally, the ironical mood is reinforced by the use of *commerce* for activities associated with love-making and by lack of a dynamic verb in the active voice—like denotes state, not activity.

Repetition and Variation lie at the root of grammatical form in poetry, and the total woven pattern is a source of formal beauty. A striking example of this basic formal feature of poetry is provided by the first verse in Part II of *Meghadutam* by Kalidas. The poet is comparing the tall palaces of Alaka with the cloud-Messenger who is directly addressed. The matching adjectives of the two nouns are very artistically arranged. The structural profile of the verse is as follows:

An_2 An_1 An_2 An_t
An_1 An_2
An_2 An_1 An_2 An_t
N_1 N_2 ...

Levin has found 'coupling' to be the cardinal mechanism in linguistic structures in poetry (1973). "Now, any two forms occurring in equivalent positions represent a pairing of convergences; only if the forms are naturally equivalent, however, do we have 'coupling', the structure that is important in poetry" (Levin 1973: 33). Levin has given, a detailed analysis of Shakespeare's "Sonnet 30".

1. When to the sessions of sweet silent thought
2. I summon up remembrance of things past,
3. I sigh the lack of many a thing I sought,
4. And with old woes new wail my dear time's waste.
5. Then can I drown an eye, unus'd to flow,
6. For precious friends hid in death's dateless night,
7. And weep afresh love's long since cancell'd woe,
8. And moan th' expense of many a vanish'd sight

9. Then can I grieve at grievances foregone,
10. And heavily from woe to woe tell o'er
11. The sad account of forebemoaned moan,
12. Which I now pay as if not paid before.
13. But if the while I think on thee, dear friend.
14. All losses are restor'd and sorrows end.

The couplings in this poem which unify it are described by Levin as follows: "*When* of line 1 and *if* of line 13 are semantically equivalent and occur in equivalent syntagmatic positions; then, in its *zero* form, at the beginning of line 3 is semantically equivalent to and occurs in the same position as *then*, again in its zero form, at the beginning of line 14" (53). Levin moves on to explore the finer details of couplings in the poem. The whole analysis is descriptively quite convincing.

Levin, however, appears to have taken liberties with the poem in its printed form and has eschewed from exploring the meaning of its grammar. He says: "constructionally, the entire sonnet consists of two conditional sentences, each one comprising a protasis and an apodosis, which we may call, respectively the condition and the conclusion. Lines 1-2 constitute the first condition, lines 3-4—extended through lines 5-12—constituted the first conclusion; line 13 constitutes the second condition, line 14 the second conclusion" (52). This framework appears to me to be inadequate for capturing all the nuances of grammatical meaning and is also at odds with the sonnet in its printed form. In its printed form the poem is composed of four sentences and in terms of thematic structure they do represent four distinct stages within two higher thought units, the first three sentences belonging to the unit first and the last sentence constituting the second unit. It will, therefore, be more helpful if we resolve the poem in the following grammatical profile, where a_1 a_2 a_3...stand for actions and e for event.

Sentence:
1. When I a_1, I a_2 and a_3
2. Then I a_4 and a_5 and a_6
3. Then I a_7 and a_8.
4. But if (the while) I a_9, e.

Now we shall see what subtle effects are achieved with the help of this grammatical structure and how the different stages of feeling are demarcated. The first two reactions of sighing and wailing, which indicate unostentatious response come instantly, almost accompany the remembrance and this is effected by the structure of the first sentence with absence of *then* before I *sigh*. The second stage clearly follows both temporally and logically because *then,* which opens line 5 has a logical colouring in view of the legal register in which the experience is coded. The activities at this stage are visible and audible reactions: *drown an eye, weep, moan*. The feeling crystallises in a concrete form involving a larger part of the personality. The next *then* (line 9), through repetition is a rhetorical intensifier and it inaugurates the third climactic stage marked by a stronger emotive reaction involving the deepest level of the personality: *grieve, from woe to woe tell o'er*. Line 13 reverses the direction of the feeling and this is signalled by but, which indicates contrast and exception. The use of *if* in line 13 as compared to *when* in line 1 is quite significant. It clearly expresses a condition: 'if during those moments of sorrow I think of you'. The result is miraculous. The instantaneous nature of relief is conveyed by zero *then* as in the first sentence. The result is an event, a revelation, which happens to the poet, without his doing anything: it is a kind of grace. The last line is couched in the syntax associated with natural process and science: passive voice and unmarked present. Strictly speaking the last line is ambiguous: Do *all* and sorrows refer to the poet's sufferings or sufferings in general. Of course the context suggests the first interpretation, but we should not forget that in Dante and in Elizabethan poetry, the beloved has something of the divine and represents the bliss giving power which destroys evil in the universe.

Let us now turn to another example of repetition and variation, the first stanza of "wants" by Phillip Larkin:

Wants

Beyond all this, the wish to be alone:
However the sky grows dark with invitation-cards
However we follow the printed directions of sex

However the family is photographed under the flagstaff
Beyond all this, the wish to be alone.

In the middle three lines, the same structure, adverbial + clause, is repeated, it has the effect of keying up the feelings higher and higher in a crescendo. However, the repetition is not an exact structural copying and significant, modulations occur within the clause as follow:

S Vint Comp
S Vt O
S V pass Adv.

The exact repetition of the first line reflects the insistence with which the desire to run away from the world of vain social activities comes back.

The ambiguity of *this* in the first line is also noticeable, what does the deictic point to and what is the effect intended? First, the poet is aware of an amorphous mass of social vanities which he ironically describes as 'wants'; they are taken cumulatively as a plethora of desires. This means the three things mentioned are to be taken as examples. Secondly, *all this* has an unpleasant tang. In common usage, when we find some activities or things unpleasant, we refer to them with *all this* as in,

What is all this?
I dislike all this.

Thus the grammatical ambiguity is employed for an exquisite effect.

Now that we have mentioned ambiguity, something more should be said about it. In poetry, ambiguity is to be taken in two senses. Literally, the term means, 'having two solutions or meanings: this sense may be extended to cover more than two meanings. We can simplify this by saying that ambiguity means, having more than one meaning.' Here is an example from "A Coat" by W.B. Yeats:

I made my song a coat

This has two meanings: 'I have a coat out of my song' and 'I made a coat for my song'. It will be seen that if we keep both the meanings in view, our reading of the poem will be enriched; and even if ultimately, we give up one of these, the ambiguity will have served its purpose. Again consider the following:

Things fall apart, the centre cannot hold.

Hold in the above line can be interpreted either as a transitive or an intransitive verb; if the former, the sense, is, 'the centre cannot hold things together' (the clause is elliptical); if in the latter case, the meaning will be, 'the centre is unable to remain in its place'. In the disruption of values being described, both the meanings are highly meaningful.

The second meaning of *ambiguity,* is 'lack of definiteness or clarity' or 'certainty'. Mystic writers in all times have made use of ambiguity in this sense in an attempt to describe what is indescribable.

नासदासीन्नो सदासीत्तदानी
नासीद्रजो नो व्योमा परो यत्

(Rig Veda)

"There was not non-existent nor the existent then; there was not the air nor the heaven which is beyond"—MacDonell. The hymn writer has described what was in the beginning by saying what it was not. Negation—morphological or syntactic—is a favourite device in such writing.

At the still point of the turning world. Neither flesh nor fleshless;
Neither from nor towards

(T.S. Eliot)

Finally, we come to the deviational meaning. Here we shall be concerned with different kinds and degrees of departure from the rules of grammar. By far the most common feature is the violation of selection or co-occurrence rules. This feature lying across the border-line of grammar and semantics, seems to be a necessary condition for poetic expression shared by the romantics and classicists alike.

Time doth transfix the flourish set on youth
And delves the parallels in beauty's brow,

Feeds on the rarities of nature's truth,
And nothing stands but for his scythe to mow,
And yet to times in hope my verse shall stand
Praising thy worth, despite his cruel hand

(Shakespeare)

In these lines a mere labelling of the main deviation as personification won't do; we'll have to explore the deviations more deeply. *Transfix, delve* and *feed* require a [+ animate] noun in the subject position, instead we have the [– animate] *time,* being led to perceive it as a destructive animal. Later when *scythe* and *hand* are attributed to it, it assumes the scope of a man. In *flourish set on youth* and *beauty's brow,* the abstract and concrete are combined to produce a striking effect. *Praising* is collocated with *verse.* The general discretion of the deviations is towards anthropomorphism which has been a major trend from the earliest times. Linguistic anthropomorphism has been the chief device of the human mind in its endeavour to grapple with and comprehend non-human reality and in older epochs it extended to all areas of knowledge including magic and primitive science. Even the rational Muse of Pope cannot help employing the device.

'Tis hard to say, if greater want of skill
Appear in writing or in judging ill;
But of the two less dangerous is the offence
To tire our patience than mislead our sense.

(Pope)

The romantic poet, however, harking back to the primitive sensibility, resorts to linguistic anthropomorphism as his anchor,

Oh there is blessing in this gentle breeze,
A visitant that while it fans my cheek
Doth seem half conscious of the joy it brings

(Wordsworth)

Another major trend is to describe humans in terms of natural objects. Let us consider the following frames:

There is a garden in her—

There is a—in her face.

In the first frame, selection rules require place-nouns, such as *town, district, compound* and in the second, such abstract nouns as *charm, beauty, defect* (although *on her face* will admit concrete nouns, e.g. *mole, spot, crack).* But whichever frame we use as the base, the following verses will be treated as deviant:

There is a garden in her face
(Where roses and white lilies blow)

(Campion)

In modern poetry de-anthropomorphism has made a conspicuous appearance, indicating an important shift in poetic sensibility. Here [+ human] items are collocated with words from the mechanical sub-register as, when a poet cries, "I am dismantled", or,

At the violet hour, when the eyes and back
Turn upward from the desk, when the human engine waits
Like a taxi throbbing waiting,

(T.S. Eliot)

The second type of grammatical deviation pertains to strict sub-categorization rules. Some clear examples are to be seen in the following lines by E.E. Cummings:

anyone lived in a pretty how town
(with up so floating many bells down)
spring summer autumn winter
he sang his didn't he danced his did.

The last line is most striking and contains the maximum grammatical deviation. The possessive *his* requires a noun; instead we get verbs. The effect is remarkable. A city dweller, living in anonymity, often talks lyrically about what he wanted to but could not do and he goes through the monotonous routine like a dancer repeating the familiar steps. The ugliness involved in both the dreams and actions of such a person are reflected in the grammatical deviations. The deviations in the first line are more complete, though grammatically they contain lesser degrees of deviation. An indefinite pronoun in the subject position would be quite in order. The deviation consists in using a non-assertive in the place of an assertive form, but the gain in meaning is substantial. First 'anyone' is more undistinguished than 'someone': the person being described could be anyone of the city crowd. Secondly, anyone is syntactically associated with negation and interrogation, which form an important aspect of the theme. This is also suggested by the second deviation: *how town*. 'How town' is a town which is incomprehensible, doesn't make sense, as it were, and raises many questions.

Dylan Thomas's phrase 'A grief ago' has often been cited as an example of deviation. Leech has discussed in a convincing way the degree of deviation involved in this expression (1969: 30-31). We shall briefly consider the meaning of the deviation. The poet is reflecting on how the woman whom he holds has mounted up the ladder of evolution. She has separated from the force which unifies man and nature; so she has not come out unscathed: she is a sinner. In a sense, the whole process of evolution is painful, it is a grief. The poet measures change in terms of the separation from the primal substance—the process of specialization. He rejects the abstract scale of time and measures evolution in terms of sorrow which is suggestive of the fall.

The kinds of grammatical deviation I have discussed do not exhaust the list. I have not mentioned, for example, deviant word order, conversion and neologism, all of which are highly meaningful in poetry. In fact the subject of deviation in poetic language has no limit, because the creative mind's ability to experiment with language is boundless. Moreover, our main aim was not to describe all the grammatical devices that are employed in poetry. Our purpose was to demonstrate the meanings which grammar contributes to the total effect produced by poetic language and I hope this aim has been achieved to some extent.

Works Cited

Langer, S. (1953). *Feeling and Form.*

Leech, G.N. (1969). *A Linguistic Guide to English Poetry.* London: Longman.

——. (1981). *Semantics,* 2nd ed. Harmondsworth: Penguin.

Leech, G.N. and M.H. Short (1981). *Style in Fiction.* London: Longman.

Levin, S.R. (1973). *Linguistic Structures in Poetry.* The Hague: Mouton.

Richards, I.A. (1926). *Principles of Literary Criticism.* Indian Rpt. 1986. Delhi: Allied Publishers.

Rodman, S. ed. (1951). "Introduction", *One Hundred Modern Poems.* New York: Mentor Books.

Sharma, R.S. (1985). *Linguistic Aspects of Contemporary English Poetry.* Varanasi: Academic Publishers.

Language and Communication

5

Considerable interest has been shown in the process of communication in recent decades as a result of what may be regarded as a technological revolution in mass-media. Whatever the variety of the media, they are all based on the process of communication. We shall therefore do well to glance at some models of communication.

Shannon and Weaver represent the process of communication in the following manner:

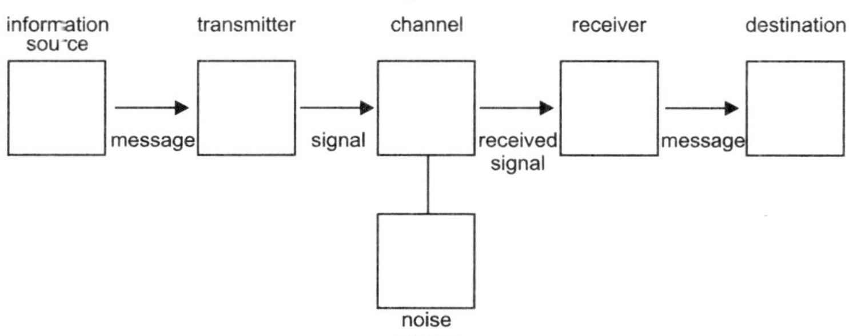

This is a mathematical model, which fails to capture all the complexities of human communication, for, we must not forget that in spite of all the technology of communication, the human factor is still a major element. Schramm, whose primary concern is with mass communication systems, offers the following model:

Language, Culture & Communication, Ed. A.K. Banerji, BHU: Faculty of Arts, 1987.

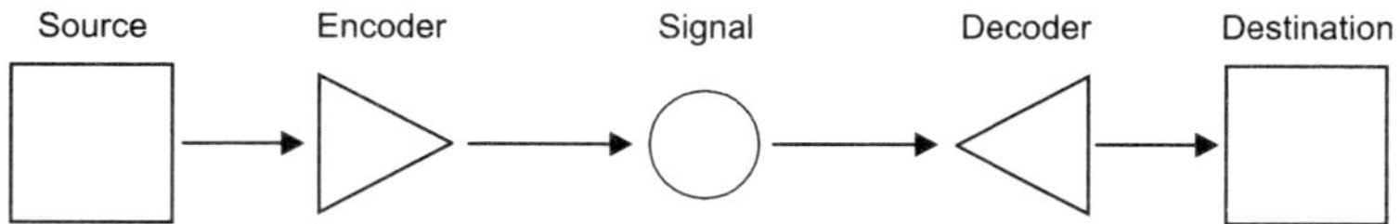

He adds, "substitute 'microphone' for encoder and 'earphone' for decoder and you are talking about electronic communication. Consider that the 'source' and 'encoder' are one person, 'decoder' and 'destination' are another, and the signal is language, and you are talking about human communication."

This model also appears to be inadequate, human communication is much more than a matter of substituting persons and language in an electronic model. The prime source of all communication is human communication; electronic communication is only an extension of and aid to human communication. A message is the product of several psychological, social and political factors combined with the unique function of the human brain, and its full meaning and purpose cannot be gathered in isolation from these factors. Imagine a girl getting this message on the telephone: 'I sha'n't be long, darling.' If she cannot identify the speaker by his or her voice quality, style and tone, she will be unable to interpret the message; it could be from her father, mother, lover or an eve-teaser. Can we think of a computerized system reporting an incident or analyzing current events?

We shall, therefore, do well to turn to a model which is based on the concept of communication as a social phenomenon. Jakobson's model was intended to explain poetic communication; nevertheless, it can equally well serve for general communication:

Context Message

Addresser • Addressee

Contact Code

Depending on the focus of orientation we get the following types of communication:

Referential

poetic

Emotive • Conative

phatic

Metalingual

These types may be treated as different functions of language. Linguists and logicians generally speak of three principal functions of language all of which are included in the above comprehensive scheme. These functions are: *informative, directive* and *expressive.* Halliday has proposed a slightly different division: according to him, again, language has three functions, but these are *ideational, interpersonal* and *textual.*

A knowledge of language functions is highly relevant to communication. It is also important to note the two principal kinds of meaning which words can have: these are *denotation* and *connotation.* Denotation is the referential meaning, the thing to which a word refers. 'Cow', for example refers to a certain animal. Connotation is the effective meaning, the feeling or emotion, a word arouses. Some words are mainly denotative, e.g. the vocabulary of science and technology and some mainly connotative, such as 'love', 'revulsion', 'sadness'.

I take the principal concern of communication to be dissemination of information. For this purpose the appropriate function of language is referential/informative/ideational. At first it may appear easy to master the use of this function, but it is not so, because, although we consider each function separately for analysis, in actual language-use, they are mixed and it requires great care and practice to achieve purely information or objective effects. Let us study the word 'cow', already cited as denotative. In addition to referring to a certain animal, it creates impressions of simplicity, harmlessness and in Hindu culture, of sanctity; we don't' associate it with food except as a source of milk. The connotation of the word to an American would be very different. As slang the word has a derogatory meaning. Similarly, 'frog' doesn't have the same range of connotation in England and France.

Journalists, sometimes unwittingly and sometimes deliberately, distort information, or create a wrong impression by means of employing unfair connotations. Take, for example, the following sentence which might appear in a report:

The area is infested with rebels.

'Rebels', of course, is to be interpreted by reference to the ruling class and we shall not say anything more about it. But what about the word 'infested'? It is not purely denotative: the verb is associated with harmful and dangerous animals and the reporter has implicitly equated the rebels with such animals, preparing the reader's mind to accept their destruction. My second example comes from an article published in *The Indian Express* of August 23, 1986:

> Mr. Atal Behari Vajpayee was on display last week in his familiar role of the man specially charged with the guardianship of national honour and dignity. And soon Mr. L.K. Advani was to add his pennyworth in the good cause.

By a subtle use of language, the author has sought to create prejudice in the reader's mind before stating the case objectively and refuting Mr. Vajpayee's assertions logically. He has made use of sarcasm and irony to denigrate the persons whose views he is going to challenge. How has it been done? Generally things are "on display", not men; the phrase has a theatrical connotation. The author has used grandiose vocabulary or which, in the present context, gives rise to irony and suggests presumption on the part of Mr. Vajpayee. "Pennyworth", again, has an unfavourable connotation.

I have said that the main task of communication (that is, mass communication) is to disseminate information. Does this mean that a communicator need have no commitment, no world-view, no framework of values?

It is impossible for a human being to be completely divested of any theory of human life and society. He is bound to adhere to one theory or another, although his commitment may be either conscious or unconscious. I do not wish to enter into the philosophy of knowing; suffice it to say that what we call objective knowledge is knowledge from the general human point of view; it has a bias towards humanity based on universal agreement. When we say that 'air pollution is harmful' is an objective statement, we unconsciously assume the human bias, for it would certainly not be so from the standpoint of anaerobic bacteria, if we can imagine them having a viewpoint.

Commitment to human interest involves another thing. The human society itself is divided into the rich and the poor, haves and have-nots, exploiter and exploited, ruling and the ruled. The former classes by their very nature are parasitic and in the minority. The latter class are productive, struggling and revolutionary, and it is to them at any particular phase of human history that progress is due. It is to the cause of these struggling masses whom we shall call the people that the journalist must be committed, for it is they who can secure the future of mankind. This approach calls for revolutionary changes in the use of language in mass-communication. This calls for a twofold struggle. First, it involves struggle against the language itself. The standard usage in the language is already biased in favour of certain classes and groups. For example, the use of pronouns and certain nouns in English reflects male domination: "all *men* are equal; if someone needs help *he* should contact the police", 'Chairman' (it is only recently that 'Chairperson' has come into greater use). Similarly the accepted meaning of such words as 'thief', 'justice' and 'democracy', show a bias in favour of the propertied class.

Secondly, the journalist has to wriggle free of the bias imposed by the ruling class through his employer, who is a member of this class. Remember that he has to use language from the standpoint of the people. This requires a courage and determination, for, whereas he has his brain all right, the means of mass-communication are in the hands of the press-baron.

Number in Hindi and Urdu: Observations on System and Context

6

Hindi and Urdu share a common grammatical structure. They both developed out of a common source, the earliest form of Hindi. Since this earliest form of Hindi preceded, most scholars believe that Urdu is an offshoot of Hindi, which grew up under Arabic and Persian influences. Platts has observed that "Urdu, or Hindustani, though a composite language, is derived mainly from Hindi" (1978, 1967: 1). Bholanath Tiwari also holds the same view on the ground that, in such matters, grammar and not vocabulary is the deciding factor (1983: 91). The actual process of Urdu's birth can be conceived in two phases. First, early Hindi, which itself had yet to develop into a full-fledged language, received the impact of Arabic and Persian in the early phase of Islamic intrusion. It borrowed a large number of foreign words and phrases and sought to accommodate them in its grammatical framework. Since Arabic, being a Semitic language, had an altogether different structure, this attempt involved an adjustment in the grammar of Hindi. New Rules, for example, had to be added to the existing ones for pluralization, although it largely meant acceptance of Arabic and Persian plurals. The noun phrase structure had also to be expanded in order to make room for

---

Read at the International Seminar on "Common Bases of Urdu and Hindi" held in the Department of Linguistics, Aligarh Muslim University.

the combination Noun + Adjective, as in *bahre Hind,* 'Indian ocean', *amīre harvā̃,* Caravan's chief.

In this phase Urdu must have been spoken as a dialect of Hindi. With further influence of foreign elements and with the association of the new dialect with a specific-speech community, Urdu developed an independent identity. This was the second phase. Urdu can, however, be regarded as an independent language with certain important qualifications. In the first place, its grammar is basically the same as that of Hindi. Secondly, its use is not confined to any particular ethnic group or geographical region. Thirdly, its chief distinguishing mark of identity is its lexicon. Fourthly, it is a part of the common heritage of our pan-Indian culture. Finally, there is, at the colloquial level, a very high degree of mutual intelligibility between Hindi and Urdu speakers—something which is rare between two languages.

With these remarks, we shall now turn to the number system as commonly shared by Hindi and Urdu. As far as nouns are concerned, number in Hindi and Urdu is involved with gender and case. The question is, what is the best method of presenting this number system? Guru, who has included the Arabic and Persian plurals in his description, believes that number should be treated separately. His main argument is that, whereas in Sanskrit, there is a distinction between the root form and the nominative singular of the noun, in Hindi there is none, and also that the changes in form which occur on account of case-inflexions can be better taken care of separately under case (1920, 1975: 175). Guru may be right, but it cannot be denied that number in Hind-Urdu is closely linked with case and it cannot be described satisfactorily without referring to case. Also, absence of root forms in Hindi is not a major obstacle. Old English, like Hindi, lacked root forms and like Hindi it also employed a reduceal case system. The grammarians of Old English, nevertheless, have managed to treat number and case together through the classical form of declension tables. The nominative singular is taken as the base form. For example, Sweet gives the following table for stān:

	Singular	*Plural*
Nominative Accousative	Stān	stān-es
Genetic	stān-es	stān-a
Dative	stān-e	stān-um

(1882, 1974: 10)

Wright and Wright go to the earlier form in which the nominative singular had *a* in the stem and treat the word under pure a-stem (1925: 175). Thus it should not be difficult to deal with number and case together in Hindi-Urdu grammar. As regards the Arabic and Persian plurals, the model can be suitably expanded so as to include them within a composite framework. Bholanath Tiwari has tabulated the plural morpheme in the context of the case particles taking õ as the basic form.

Morpheme	Allomorph		
õ	1.	-õ̃	With postposition in all words.
	2.	-õ	In the vocative in all words.
	3.	-é	In the absence of postposition with masculine nouns ending in *ā*.
	4.	-ẽ̃	In the absence of postposition with feminine nouns ending in a consonant, *ā*, u, ū, or *au*.
	5.	-ā̃	In the absence of postposition with nouns ending in *i*, *ī* or *iya*.
	6.	- ∅	In the absence of postposition with masculine nouns ending in a consonant, *i*, *ī*, *u* or *ū*.

(1983: 231)

The above classification is based on gender form of the stem and presence or absence of postposition. We can go a step further and present the number system (including the singular) along with case. This will perhaps simplify the description and make it more systematic as well as pedagogically useful. Fairbanks and Misra have noted that nouns in Hindi are inflected for two cases: nominative and oblique (1966: 50). The description given by Bhoblanatha Tiwari shows that we must also consider the vocative separately. This will lead to the construction of declension tables for various groups of nouns under each gender. We give some examples.

1. Masculine nouns ending in ā:

Larkā, 'boy'

	Singular	*Plural*
Nominative	larka	larkē
Oblique	larke	lark ȭ
Vocative	larke	larko

2. Masculine nouns ending in a consonant:

Bālak, 'boy'

	Singular	*Plural*
Nominative	bālak	bālak
Oblique	bālak	bālak ȭ
Vocative	balak	bālakō

3. Feminine nouns ending in a consonant:

Kitāb, 'book'

Nominative	kitāb	kitābẽ̄
Oblique	kitāb	kitāb ȭ
Vocative	kitāb	kitābē

This kind of tabulation will enable us to set down the plural morpheme and its allomorphs very neatly; it will also reveal the number system more clearly.

So far we have been concerned mainly with the broad outline of number system employed in both Hindi and Urdu. At the colloquial level, the tendency to depend on this broad pattern appears to be on the increase. However, since Arabic and Persian plurals continue to be used, it is necessary to account for them. One way to do so is to give the rules for the formation of such plurals separately and this is what Guru has done (1975: 179-81). Platts gives a more detailed account of Arabic plurals (1967: 102-12). The question is how to integrate these plurals into the broad framework shared by Hindi and Urdu. This is necessary in view of the fact that the native Hindi rules and those of Arabic and Persian form a composite system applied by Hindi and Urdu speakers alike: it is actually part of their competence. Also, a great majority of Urdu nouns of Arabic and Persian origin make two plurals: one according to the native rules of Hindi and the other according to the grammar of their language of origin somewhat modified. These considerations call for an expansion of the tables and for providing additional rules. Let us take up two examples:

Saḥib, 'gentleman, officer'.

	Singular	*Plural*
Nominative	sahib	sāhib sāhibān
Oblique	sāhib	sāhib ȭ sāhibān
Vocative	sāhib	sāhib(ō) sāhibān

We shall add a sub-rule to say that a group of animate nouns headed by Sahib form alternative plurals with the suffix *an* and also a general note that, where two plurals are available, the choice of one or the other is a matter of style and context.

2. Lafẓ, 'word'

	Singular	*Plural*
Nominative	lafẓ	lafẓ airāẓ
Oblique	lafẓ	laf z̄ọ alfāẓ
Vocative	lafẓ	lafẓ(ō) alfāẓ

Words of the above type will require a substantial addition involving the introduction of infixes and therefore, an expansion of the basic number system of Hindi.

Hindi and Urdu also share a common stock of case particles, generally called postpositions. They pattern with specific forms of the noun to convey case relations other than nominative and vocative. The principal case particles are *nẽ*, *kō, sē, kā-kē-kī,* and *mẽ*. Of these, the genitive marker is inflected for gender, and for number in the masculine gender.

We shall forbear going into further complexities of the composite number system. Instead, we now take up the question of choice from the alternative plurals. Arabic and Persian plurals are used, as a rule, in the legal language irrespective of whether it is written in *devanagari* or Arabic script. The following words have been picked up at random from a legal document: *śarāyat, hakūk, tamīrāt, hālāt, umūr, savālat, dastavezāt.* Literary and technical Urdu also abound in Arabic and Persian plurals. The situation is comparable to that of English. In legal and technical English, foreign plurals are chosen, as a rule, although in colloquial and other varieties of English the *-s* plurals predominate. Some of the examples are *antennae* (in Zoology, but *antennas* in radio communication), *formulae, indices, media.* Some Arabic plurals have developed a new meaning with a singular sense, such as *akḥabār* ('newspaper') and tawārikh (history). In such cases the native plural is preferred: *khabarē, tārīkhē.*

The most interesting phenomenon is the choice of plurals as a matter of social courtesy or politeness strategy. In order to understand this phenomenon, we must take notice of the fact that the native speakers of Hindi and Urdu possess in common a certain stock of both kinds of Plurals and have perfomative competence to use one or the other; further, the native speakers of Hindi normally employ the nativised plurals and those of Urdu make use of Arabic and Persian plurals. Secondly, Urdu as a native tongue is associated in the public mind, with the Muslim community and, although, this is not a fact, that public psychology can be seen to be an important factor in linguistic courtesy. For example, it has been pointed out that when a Hindu visits a Muslim family he tends to use the Urdu forms of salutation and parting; similarly when a Muslim goes to a Hindu's house, he is inclined to employ Hindi forms. The main point is that this kind of linguistic behaviour is not confined to phatic expressions; it extends to vocabulary as well as the plural forms. A Hindu talking to a Muslim is likely to use *hālat, alfāz, umra, hukkām,* etc., whereas a Muslim conversing with a Hindu will simplify them to *hulato, lafzo, amiro,* hakimo, etc. It is significant to note that when a Hindu talks to another Hindu who is Urdu speaking, he does not feel the need of making the above-mentioned concession. Another point worth-noting is that the native speaker of Hindi in this kind of interaction shares only a part of the Urdu speaker's competence: his knowledge of Arabic and Persian plurals is very limited; the Urdu speaker suffers from no such handicap in the use of the nativised plural forms of Arabic and Persian words. In conclusion, it may be said that the minor sociolinguistic detail we have just noted is a sign of the great cultural and social adjustment which the two speech communities have achieved in the course of their long stay together. There are many other such interlingual phenomena which betray the spirit of synthesis and goodwill between the two communities, e.g. Indianisation of Persian derivational suffixes and adoption of Arabic and Persian phrasal expressions. They represent the harmony of social relations between the two communities and give a lie to the hoarse cries of the prophets of discord.

Works Cited

Bholanath Tiwari (1983). *Hindi Bhasa.* Allahabad: Kitab Mahal.

Gordon H. Fairbanks (1966) and Bal Govind Misra (1966). *Spoken and Written Hindi.* New York: Cornell University Press.

John T. Platts (1967). *A Grammar of the Hindustani or Urdu Language.* Delhi: Munshiram Manoharlal.

J. Wright and E.H. Wright (1925). *Old English Grammar.* London: Oxford University Press.

Kamata Prasad Guru (1975). *Hindi Vyakarana.* Varanasi: Nagaripracarini Sabha.

Sweet (1982). *Anglo-Saxon Primer* (Revised by N. Davis, 1974). London: Oxford University Press.

Technical Style: Implications of Operationalism

7

A static view of technical style is represented by its description in terms of the choice of certain distributional features such as the unmarked present, the agentless passive, functional use of the pronouns *we* and *you* and technical vocabulary. Textbook writers on technical English called the appropriate style 'impersonal style' and proceeded to offer advice on how to achieve it. Woolley has distinguished 'personal' and 'impersonal' styles with the examples, *I filled the test tube with water* and *the test tube was filled with water* adding 'the impersonal style is more suitable for technical or scientific description'. Authors have adduced plausible reasons for the use of impersonal style in scientific and technical texts. M.P. Dresdner justifies the use of the passive voice on the ground that 'scientific texts generally place the emphasis on what happens to *things* instead of on the *person* who performs the action'. In my book on *Technical Writing* I have related the impersonal style to the attitude of the scientist and the nature of his subject matter and have named passive construction, functional use of the pronouns 'we' and 'you' and description words as its chief features. In a similar vein G.W. Turner has observed:

> But Science must be 'invariant to all observers' and experiments, not experimenters, were the centre of interest. This encourages an impersonal style, that is, in

IDELTI Journal, Vol. 18 (Baghdad), 1981.

relation to the general language, a third person style. If the scientist must mention himself, he calls himself 'the present writer', but he is seldom present at all.

A further point implied in the above discussion and made explicit by T.H. Savory in his detailed treatment of scientific language is the fixity of technical language. Although technical style involves choice, for there may be non-technical ways of saying the same thing, within itself it offers no scope for variation. In science, says Savory just as the one word has, or should have, one meaning only, so also there is usually only one way in which to express any particular meaning. Even so simple a sentence as 'Total internal reflection occurs if the angle of incidence is greater than the critical angle', cannot, I think, be expressed in any other words, except of course, by using absurd explanatory periphrases. The approach outlined above possessed a high degree of self assurance and it seemed impossible to characterise technical style in any other way. Yet both the style itself and the basic philosophical assumptions underlying it have been challenged. My aim is to consider some of the objections to the conventional methods of scientific expression, as stated or implied in "operationalism".

M.A.K. Halliday *et al.* have made a pertinent remark in *The Linguistic Sciences and Language Teaching*: "The planned development of scientific registers is an important task of applied linguistics, and must be treated as such; it could be successful only if worked out by scientists and linguists in collaboration." Fortunately, like philosophers, scientists have lately evinced a good deal of interest in examining the kind of 'reality' they deal with and the linguistic tools used to express it. They have begun analysing language in their own way to test its ability and limitation as a carrier of scientific message.

Scientist's concern with language is part of his philosophical preoccupation, his attempt to understand the logical and cognitive aspects of scientific knowledge. A major movement among scientists called 'operationalism' or 'operationism' has questioned the certainties and objectivity of classical science and has picked logical holes in its permanent looking facade; it insists on defining scientific concepts in terms of identifiable and repeatable operations and holds that the meaning of a scientific term or preposition consists of the operation or operations performed in defining or demonstrating it. In order to appreciate the shift in attitude and manner of expression necessitated by operationalism, it seems desirable to me to consider the doctrine in some detail.

Operationalism traces its origin in Einstein's theory of relativity. Einstein had showed that if someone says that two events took place at the same time, he is, strictly speaking, making a meaningless statement because two events which appear to be simultaneous to one observer may not be so from the standpoint of another observer. The results propounded by Einstein jeopardised the assumption of absolute time and, in general, the objectivity of scientific knowledge by calling attention to the uniqueness of observer and frame of reference. "The operationist thesis is that every specific concept must be connected to experience by means of precisely given operations, which tell us how to apply the concept" (John G. Kemeny). Inclusion of observer and framework as integral parts of the total situation in scientific observation and experiment, and the realisation that the ultimate sources of cognition are the senses, although greatly assisted by instruments, relate operationalism, to empiricism. "Operationalists", says Kemeny, "argue that all useful concepts must originate from experience as well, and hence require operational definitions for all theoretical concepts". Operational approach to knowledge is based on the assumption that "all theoretical terms of any science whatever are reducible to descriptions of the operation or procedures of measurement, so that measurement statements themselves are reduced to descriptions of the experimental procedures in terms of which such measurements take place" (M.W. Wartofsky).

P.W. Bridgman, a foremost advocate of operationalism, in his *The Way Things Are* has thrown the doctrine in sharp relief and has also discussed its relation to the nature of experience on the one hand and language on the other. We must, therefore, consider his views at some length.

In the Preface of the book Bridgman informs us that in the course of time the importance of the individual became increasingly obvious to him even in science which is sometimes actually defined in social, public terms, adding, "My reason for insisting on the importance of the role of individual in science was that 'proof', without which no science is possible, is entirely an affair of the individual and is therefore private, with the result that any creative science is of necessity private rather than public." This turning of the scale convinced him of the necessity of first person report, if immediate experience was 'to be communicated with any faithfulness or freshness'. Generally, operational analysis is "a particular case of analysis in terms of activities—doings or happenings". The author became convinced in the course of his practice along this line, of the superiority of analysis in terms of doings or happenings rather than objects or static abstractions. This is undoubtedly a new and unusual approach. The attempt to see things in terms of activities demands the use of the first person, since the performer of an operation cannot be dispensed with. "When I make a statement, even as coldly and impersonal a statement as a proposition of Euclid it is I that am making the statement, and the fact that it is I that am making the statement is part of the picture of the activity."

Operational procedure according to Bridgman has brought another important insight—the insight that we can never get away from ourselves not only as individuals but also as human race. He hints at the contradiction involved in the accessibility of purely objective knowledge as it is impossible to examine 'reality' from the outside since "the brain that tries to understand is itself part of the world that it is trying to understand". Thus what we call objectivity is no more than the other pole of subjectivity.

Words are associated with meaning through activities and without considering operations we cannot arrive at the exact meaning of words. Meaning is not so public as it is supposed to be; the background of the operator and the time of operation are vital elements in the communication of meaning. In identification and meaning of words we cannot discount "the brains of the people that use the word". The printed word in isolation does not mean something, it is the user who means something. Emphasis on the activity aspect of the word demands that this not be lost sight of. A simple verbal trick is helpful in this connection. Never ask "What does word X mean?" but ask instead "what do I mean when I say word X?" or "What do you mean when you say word X?" Knowing the meaning of a word is being able to state the conditions of its use by you or by me.

We need not overemphasize the role of the operator, for in science as Bridgman has admitted we deal with 'classes' of operations and we drop the operator and time where they do not make any difference. But we have to be very cautious in this respect. "Although most specifications of scientific operations are given in impersonal terms in the sense that no explicit mention is made of the performer, a performer is nevertheless pretty close." In the author's view there are situations in physics "in which the performer of the operations is an essential part of the picture although his role is concealed". Situations of this sort are presented by general relativity theory or by the "general cosmological principle".

The role of situational elements including operator depends on the 'level of operation' which itself, for Bridgman, appears to be based on degree of objectivity. "There is in the first place the almost completely public 'objective' level of classical physics, chemistry and the other non-biological science. On this level we pay no attention to the performer of the operations, as such, and do not talk about feeling or thinking." Bridgman places mathematics on a level of lower 'objectivity' than physics or chemistry because for him, in mathematics proof is largely 'a personal matter'. Similarly logic. The biological sciences are put on the next level, and within this level "there is a hierarchy of such sciences, perhaps beginning with descriptive botany and culminating in human psychology". This level is followed by the level of social phenomena. "The operations which give meaning to many social concepts involve in many cases the performer of the operations. For instance, the law that is 'social law' as distinguished from 'natural' law is a body of permitted practice, originating in specific ways in the activities of certain individuals who are designated as competent to make laws, and enforced by other individuals also specially designated."

In his discriminating analysis of various sciences which fills the bulk of the books Bridgman discovers the role of the performer in unsuspected places and finds justification for the use of 'introspectional words' in many situations in only the operator's 'private aspect'. "Such usage is consistent with the vision that I cannot get away from myself. Because of this, any 'ultimate true' account that I can give of the world has to be from myself as centre—any valid report has to be reducible to the first person singular if it is not actually already in the first person. In order to give this first person account with the greatest vividness and immediacy I find it almost unavoidable to use such words as 'think' and 'feel' and 'remember' and 'conscious' in describing my direct experience, that is, to use these words in their private aspect." What are the implications of this operationalism for technical style as practised and taught at present? First, it undermines a static and mechanical concept of a single manner of expression in terms of prescribing a few selected grammatical and lexical features with a view to achieving the so-called impersonal style. Ultimately all scientific knowledge is referable to human experience and a faithful communication of experience demands greater flexibility and a more liberal use of the linguistic resources than is permitted by the do's and don'ts of the conventional style. The supremacy of unmarked present and the agentless passive is automatically reduced to size. Second, instead of a single uniform style, a broad stylistic range is suggested and a careful choice of stylistic features is demanded to suit the nature of a particular science: in psychology, for example, maximum communication efficiency cannot be attained without using 'introspectional words' and a faithful report of an experiment can be written only in the first person. Third, by drawing attention to the totality of the situation, specially to the importance of operator and time as well as the dynamic nature of operations, the conventional restriction on the use of full pronominal and tense systems of English is removed. The use of 'I' and of 'we' and 'you' in a personal sense is not only permissible but also desirable in some situations, so is the use of the past and future tenses as well as different modals. Last, the operational approach has reduced the vast gap between technical and common style in terms of the range of grammatical structure although in terms of frequency distributions and vocabulary the two remain clearly distinct.

Works Cited

Bridgman, P.W. *The Way Things Are.* Harward University Press, 1959.

Dresdner, M.P. "Teaching Scientific English", *English Teaching Forum,* Vol. XIII, No. 3 and 4, 1975.

Halliday, M.A.K., McIntosh, A. and Strevens, P. *The Linguistic Sciences and Language Teaching.* E.L.B.S., 1964.

Kemeny, J.G. *A Philosopher Looks at Science.* D. Van Nostrand Company, 1959.

Savory, T.H. *The Language of Science.* Andre Deutsch, 1967.

Sharma, R.S. *Technical Writing* Part I. Tara Publications, Varanasi, 1971.

Turner, G.W. *Stylistics.* Penguin Books, 1973.

Wartofsky, M.W. *Conceptual Foundations of Scientific Thought,* The Macmillan Company, 1968.

Woolley, J.G. *English for the Technical Student.* Taraporevala.

Review –1

8

Geoffrey N. Leech and Michael H. Short. *Style in Fiction: A Linguistic Introduction to English Fictional Prose.* London: Longman, 1981. XIII + 402.

This book offers an excellent and up-to-date introduction to stylistics and the linguistic study of English fictional prose. In certain respects, however, it does not entirely fulfil the expectations raised by its main title.

From beginning to end, the book displays the clarity and systematic organisation characteristic of Leech's writings. The authors have adopted a very sensible and practical approach to most issues. Unlike J.P. Thorne, and some others, they regard literary language as a special exploitation of the structure of language, rather than a 'dialect' to be described or learnt separately (1, 5-6). This is a sound view. It enables the analyst-interpreter to describe the novelist's linguistic manipulations against the general background of the structure of a language. It also denies a water-tight division between common English and literary English for such a division is, in fact, non-existent. Strictly speaking there is no literary language; there are literary uses of language. This view is particularly relevant to the study of the novel, which seeks to represent reality. The authors have given a clear and concise account of 'style' and 'stylistics', the various meanings attached to the term 'style', and the relation between content and style. The controversy regarding form and content is well-known in both literary theory and stylistics.

IRAL, XXI/4 (1983).

Leech and Short have carefully weighed the merits and demerits of 'monism' and 'dualism' and have adapted Halliday's functional model to develop their own multilevel approach (34-38, Ch. 4). This is a very satisfactory solution both theoretically and practically. The model is, however, tentative and a distinct system of stylistic levels does not emerge. 'Stylistically', the framework offered by Crystal and Davy, although not completely satisfactory, seems better. It enables us to assign grammatical features to what they call 'dimensions of situational constraint', e.g. individuality, monologue, singularity. This model can take account of authorial, period and genre styles, but it is less developed than the model presented by Leech and Short.

It is a very sane view to state that stylistics "cannot be reduced to mechanical objectivity" (4). Quantitative studies have certainly yielded some remarkable results, but in these studies it is not the data which has 'spoken'. Important stylistic conclusions, even analysis in a particular direction, have been most often preceded by a hunch felt after some preliminary study. Some of the statements, however, fail to convince; for example, the view that cohesion is "not always an important aspect of literary style" (254). On the other hand, a thorough study of 'Connection' can provide a key to the novelist's conception of reality and his artistic intention. Louis T. Milic's investigation of Swift's writings reveals that the way Swift uses conjunctions and related words is a fundamental aspect of his work. It should be conceded here that Cohesion (also Coherence) as used in literature has not been fully described; it is more complex than the work of Widdowson and Halliday and Hasan would suggest.

Another merit of the book is a full coverage of the areas of stylistics the authors have chosen for treatment. The first two chapters discuss the concept of style and the business of stylistics, Chapter 3 presents a method of analysis, Chapter 4 is concerned with levels of style and the whole of Part II deals with a variety of vital issues pertaining to the language and techniques of fictional writing. The description of 'mind style' through close linguistic analysis is remarkable; the discussion and interpretation of the passages is masterly. The authors should have devoted more space and expended more scholarship on 'point of view', which is a cardinal concept in fiction criticism: Henry James gave considerable importance to the topic, and according to Percy Lubbock it governs "the whole intricate question of method". Broadly defined, 'point of view' would cover nearly all aspects of a novel and can offer a clue to its artistic form.

The authors deserve commendation for incorporating in their framework the recent insights offered by discourse analysis, speech-act theory, linguistic theory and fiction criticism. Their examination of different modes of speech, e.g. 'free direct speech', 'narrative report of speech-acts' and their stylistic significance, and the description of the mechanism of narration are extremely valuable for understanding fictional technique. This part of the book will also be helpful in interpreting individual works of fiction.

The book is complete in all important respects, as a first course. The passages and topics supplied for further study are quite suitable and the questions asked are both crucial and stimulating. Under "Further Reading" the authors have provided expert guidance on the literature in the area.

The major contribution of Leech and Short is found in Chapter 3, where they present a detailed method for the linguistic analysis of a passage. Their approach to analysis is the only one feasible at the present stage. "There is no infallible technique for selecting what is significant. We have to make ourselves newly aware, for each text, of the artistic effect of the whole, and the way linguistic details fit into the whole" (74-75). They have neatly divided the task under four general headings: lexical categories, grammatical categories, figures of speech, cohesion and context. The analytical apparatus is comprehensive and fine enough to capture nearly every fact of stylistic importance. The checklist of linguistic and stylistic categories poses questions that can draw out literary implications. They have analysed in detail single paragraphs from Joseph Conrad, D.H. Lawrence, and Henry James and their discussion of the stylistic features of these passages is highly competent. Fiction-stylistic, however, is much more than the study of single paragraphs. The paragraph may be a unit of the text and anlysis will certainly lead to a full interpretation of it, but a paragraph (even the opening paragraph) is not a constituent of the design of a novel as a work of art. We cannot draw truly important stylistic conclusions from such analysis regarding, for example, the nature, type, or constituent structure of the plot; it is not possible to establish a relation between the linguistic organisation and the literary form. There is no denying the fact that such analysis is a necessary first step in every type of stylistic study and to this extent Leech and Short have rendered valuable service to fiction stylistics. Yet much has remained unattempted.

The authors should have added a separate chapter discussing at least one whole novel. This could have been done by drawing upon the full studies made by others. Both Henry James, a novelist, and Ullmann, a stylistician, have insisted on this. According to the latter, any study of a stylistic device is useless unless it examines the entire work of art. The main task is to attack the novelistic form from the linguistic end. And this is what Roger Fowler has attempted in his *Linguistics and the Novel.* His theory states that texts are structurally similar to sentences, and at the same time, they are constructed out of sentences. (I do not think that the theory is successful but that is another matter.) In another direction, several authors have presented stylistic studies of individual novels or novelists, and their findings have led to fresh insights into the form and meaning of the novels and the artistic personality of the novelists concerned.

To be just to the authors, they have stated that they will not discuss authorial, genre and period style (6) but in doing so they have left largely untouched the most central concerns of fiction stylistics and restricted the usefulness and range of their analytical apparatus.

These remarks must not be allowed to detract from the merit of the book. As an introduction to the analysis of the language of fiction and to its linguistic aspects, e.g., different modes of narration, the work is very useful and highly successful.

Works Cited

Booth, Wayne C. *The Rhetoric of Fiction*. Chicago: The University of Chicago Press, 1961.

Crystal, D. and Davy, D. *Investigating English Style*. London: Longman, 1969.

Fowler, R. *Linguistics and the Novel*. London: Methuen, 1977.

Halliday, M.A.K. and Hasan, R. *Cohesion in English*. London: Longman, 1976.

James, Henry. *The Art of the Novel*, ed. R.P. Blackmur. New York: Scribner's, 1934.

Lodge, D. *Language of Fiction*. London: Routledge and Kegan Paul, 1966.

Lubbock, P. *The Craft of Fiction* (1921). London: Jonathan Cape, 1955.

Milic, Louis T. *A Quantitative Approach to the Style of Jonathan Swift*. The Hague: Mouton, 1967.

Schorer, Mark. "Technique as Discovery" in *20th Century Literary Criticism*, ed. Lodge D. London: Longman, 1972.

Thorne, J.P. "Generative Grammar and Stylistic Analysis" in *New Horizons in Linguistics*, ed. Lyons, John. Harmondsworth: Penguin, 1970.

Ullmann, S., *Style in the French Novel*. London: Oxford University Press, 1957.

Wellek, Rene and Warren, Austin. *Theory of Literature* (1949), Harmondsworth: Penguin, 1963.

Widdowson, H.G. "Discourse" in *Teaching Language as Communication*, Oxford: Oxford University Press, 1978.

Review–2

9

Walter Nash. *The Language of Humour: Style and Technique in Comic Discourse*. London and New York: Longman, 1985. XIV + 181.

Humour is a serious matter, when you come to think of it; in the final analysis it is as elusive as tragedy. Man is the only laughing animal, but why does he laugh? We cannot proceed without devising a working definition of the Comic. From a linguistic point of view, Crystal and Davy (1969: 78-81) have hinted at the problems involved in describing literature and humour. Humour requires a double theory: epistemological and linguistic. Nash could certainly have offered a better perspective on humour, had he included an introductory chapter on the nature of Comic discourse. Thinkers from Aristotle down to Bergson and beyond have directly or indirectly recognized 'playful distortion' as the basic factor in humour. This distortion may be effected in reality (through the power of the Comic imagination), in logic, or in any or all of the language components: phonology, morphology, syntax and semantics. Nash's book does richly illustrate the phenomenon, but without a unifying theory. The author has also not taken into account work done in discourse analysis, particularly by Sinclair and Coulthard (1975) and Leech and Short (1981) with the result that the hierarchical units (if any) set up by him have failed to crystallize: the 'humoureme' has eluded him.

IRAL, XXIV/4 (1986).

The book, nevertheless, comprehends the whole range of Comic discourse extending from aphorisms and jokes to humorous stories, novels, rhimes and doggerels. Nash has rightly and most convincingly demonstrated the need for explaining a joke, laying bare the various strands involved—cultural and linguistic (Chapter One). In Chapter Two, we are told, "metaphors that link laughter and explosiveness ('erupt', 'burst out') touch on an interesting paradox: that the energies of humour, like those of a detonation, are both contractive and expansive" (13).

The two processes of witty compression and comic expansion are fully discussed with appropriate examples. The next two chapters attempt a systematic description of the structure, or design, of jokes in terms of their forms and components. The concept of 'locus' is a valuable one. I think a deeper linguistic analysis of jokes would yield yet another element which may be called 'release'. The release can be physically verified by the onset of laughter. Locus and release perhaps coincide in some aphoristic jokes. Take the following example:

> Elderly Woman: Mary, it's time you found a husband.
>
> Mary: (after some deliberation) Whose do you suggest?

Here *husband* is the locus and *whose,* the release. I remember a friend having prefaced his joke by remarking that we would laugh six times, and, indeed, all of us did.

Nash has rightly devoted one full chapter to the discussion of allusion and parody, since they account for a large proportion of Comic discourse. His own parody of Hopkins' style is hilarious (82-83). In Chapters six and seven, the author deals with manipulations of logic and meaning respectively. His semantic exploration of humorous language is both scholarly and interesting. However, he ought to have paid special attention to register-mixing, which is demonstrably an important device used in comic discourse (Halliday, *et al.* 1964: 88). Similarly literalism also deserves a separate mention. In the last chapter, Nash has competently dealt with rhyme, rhythms and various kinds of frames employed in comic discourse. The Bibliography is highly useful, although some brief comments on humour to be found in works on linguistics, stylistics and discourse analysis have not been included.

Humour is a means of survival in a social group; it is used both as an offensive and a defensive weapon. People daily create humour of their own with or without the help of available stock, in order to save or face a situation. During a political trial in India, the accused said "There is an Arabic proverb which says 'always consult your wife but do what you think best' (laughter). I think that is the law in regard to assessors also (laughter). Always consult your wife, that is the assessor, but do what you, the Judge, think best [laughter]" (Noorani 1978: 177). One would have liked such data included and analysed.

Considering the difficulties involved in such an enterprise, Nash's book is a pioneering contribution to the linguistic study of humour. Some of his categories and classes, however, remain tentative, but this cannot be avoided since discourse analysis itself is in its infancy and cannot altogether be prevented from pressing at improper places—*infancy* is the locus and pressing, a double release.

Works Cited

Crystal, D. and Davy, D. *Investigating English Style*. London: Longman, 1969.

Halliday, M.A.K., McIntosh, A. and Strevens, P. *The Linguistic Sciences and Language Teaching*. London: ELBS and Longman, 1964.

Leech, G.N. and Short, M. *Style in Fiction*. London: Longman, 1981.

Noorani, A.H. *Indian Political Trials*. Delhi: Sterling Publishers, 1978.

Sinclair, J. McH. and Coulthard, R.M. *Towards an Analysis of Discourse*. London: Oxford University Press, 1975.

Part - II
Language Teaching

The Teaching of Technical English in Indian Context

10

The teaching of English in the Indian context is an extremely complicated job with a variety of problems including the linguistic ones. In India we have a broad spectrum of linguistic background, comprising four language families, more than a dozen major languages and scores of dialects. English itself continues in everyday use in many homes, but it is not the same as Standard British English.

The multilingual context offers a variety of problems to the teacher of English, some of which are of considerable interest to the linguist. One of the well attested phenomena is L_t (mother tongue) interference at all levels, phonological, grammatical and semantic. In the teaching of Technical English (TE), a further source of interference has been noticed. It is what may be called 'Common English' (CE). In the following discussion we will consider the above two kinds of interference under the name 'double interference'.

Before the double interference phenomena can be investigated, it is necessary to distinguish between Common and Technical English, a point often missed by the teacher.

We may designate TE as a 'register' of the English language with special phonological, grammatical and semantic features. The general linguistic structure is the same, yet the rules of the language operate in a special way in TE. A.J. Herbert, in the

IRAL, Vol. XVI/2 (1978).

Preface to his practice book, *The Structure of Technical English* (1965) has remarked that "the language in which scientific and technical facts are expressed is certainly not a different language from that of everyday life, but all the same it presents the foreign student with a number of special problems".

Generally speaking, technical language is a form of language used for transmission, in a systematized manner, of a particular branch of specialized knowledge pertaining to nature and conditions of life. It is thus relevant as much to law and philosophy as to electronics and biology. The aim of technical language is to present knowledge in a series of objective, direct and unambiguous statements. It is chiefly concerned with facts and underlying principles, as poetry is with moods and affective states of the mind. Ambiguity of symbols and utterances may, if used properly, help the poet create the desired, often undefinable feeling, but in technical expression there can be no greater bane.

As already stated, on the whole, the laws of a language apply throughout the material expressed by its medium. Yet, according to the aims of different kinds of writing, the operation and distribution of linguistic features may change. Certain aspects of the language may become more important in one than in the other. An obvious distinguishing characteristic for example, of technical language is set terminology or 'technical vocabulary'. Certain words here assume peculiar importance for a particular discipline, and their grammatical and semantic 'behaviour' in the technical register is different from that in the common parlance.

In the author's view, all technical expression, because of a single common aim, namely, communication of information in clear, unambiguous terms, follows certain broad principles, irrespective of the subject-matter expressed, but in the present paper, we will use the term 'technical language' or 'technical English' for the register employed in the 'texts' of science and technology.

Technical English has several distinguishing features at every level of the linguistic structure. It is a formal variety of the language used for specific expression and not for meeting situations in everyday life. The phonological, grammatical and semantic patterns of English are selectively and adaptively used to attain direct, definite and detached expression.

We can here mention only a few of the distinguishing features of TE:

(i) *Phonology:* In the first place there are hundreds of technical terms composed of unfamiliar Greek and Latin elements seldom heard by the common user of English. The correct pronunciation of such terms has to be learned separately. Their polysyllabic word patterns are in contrast with the mono and dissyllabic ones of colloquial English. One might consider, for example, the words, *achondroplasiac, calyptobranchiate, Chorioallantoic.* Secondly, many obvious features of colloquial English such as contracted forms, e.g. *hasn't, won't* are not commonly found in TE. Thirdly, the complex intonation of English is only partially used in TE. The full scale of international variations related to meaningful distinctions in feeling, mood, and attitude is not needed in an impersonal kind of speech.

(ii) *Grammar*: In CE compounds are made by putting two or more words together which in most cases can be recognised, as in *life-sketch, boat-house.* In Technical English the favourite method of compounding is the merging of two or more Greek or Latin elements into a single word as in *biology, photosynthesis,* and *trigonometry.* Thus in the morphology of Technical English mastery of what may be called the 'building bricks' and rules of their combination is essential. We also have unique forms by conversion, e.g., *transform,* used as a noun.[1] Second, 'irregular pluralization' is a minor matter in CE, but in TE it is an important feature, because, a great majority of terms, drawn from the classical languages as they are, form their plurals according to the rules of the parent language. It would therefore be more appropriate to call the process 'classical plural'. Among the chief syntactic features of Technical English are the use of neutral Present, Passive construction without Agentive Phrase, Conditional Clause and a general lack of those patterns which are common in familiar dialogue, e.g., Question Tags and Exclamations.

(iii) *Semantics:* The semantic 'sets' and 'fields' of Technical English are well marked and distinct from those of common English. Familiar words such as *force, work, power* and *mixture* have 'defined' meanings. For example, *ambiguity* has no ambiguity of meaning in Trigonometry as it has its original meaning, i.e., 'going in both ways', as in 'the ambiguous case' where two triangles can be drawn from the same data.

The proper style for technical expression is 'impersonal'. It is achieved in English by the use of purely descriptive terms and set formal phrases, functional use of pronouns *we* and *you* and what has been called 'impersonal passive'.

Finally, it must be noted that TE uses mathematical symbols and formulae as an integral part of the communication system. Mathematics itself has close affinity with language and its exact symbolization of relationships and results contributes to the definiteness of expression.

TE, it might be clear now, is a specialized form of the English language with typical phonological, grammatical and semantic features superposed on the general linguistic system of English. This differentiation has important contrastive implications insofar as a foreign user of TE is concerned. In his use of TE we can predict two sources of interference: mother tongue and CE. In the following paragraphs we shall illustrate 'double interference' chiefly from the data collected in the course of teaching TE at the Institute of Technology, Banaras Hindu University. Whenever necessary, tests and exercises were specially designed to suit the purpose. Most of the observations are related to Hindi-speaking students.

In Pronunciation, L_1 interference continues to operate. In technical communication, as in colloquial English, students from the Eastern region often fail to distinguish between /i/ and /i:/. The same group uses /s/ and /S/ indiscriminately and the error is reflected in writing in such sentences as, "a catalysis in shape is smooth, shoft and colourless" (Bengali).

But a different kind of errors is found in the following:

1. But it doesn't change. (Telugu)
2. If one didn't react with the other. (Punjabi)
3. Every reaction hasn't got the same rate (Hindi).

The use of contracted forms is odd from the TE point of view and the source of the error is not L_1. We find students with different language backgrounds using the contracted forms. Also the practice of contracted forms is a major concern in colloquial English. It is, therefore, reasonable to conclude that the interference in this case is from CE and not from L_1. The conclusion is confirmed when we find a Thai speaking student saying, "and the final action won't change the substance...."

Sentence (3) above, in *hasn't got,* shows grammatical interference from CE. Another example is the use of phenomena as a singular noun by several students. The 'habitual' logic behind the error seems to lie in the assumption that the plural of a noun ends in a sibilant. The obverse of this, noted commonly, is the addition of a sibilant suffix instead of classical plural e.g. *funguses, *supernovas. The following analogical errors also came to notice:

4. They accelerate or *deaccelerate* the velocities of chemical reaction. (Hindi)
5. The reaction is accelerated or *retardated.* (Hindi)

Semantic interference from CE is attested in the form of the use of a colloquial or emotive word where TE would expect a descriptive or technical one. The following examples may be noted:

6. But according to another theory the reactants *gather* on the catalyst. (Hindi)
7. In chemistry we define catalysis as a process by which the rate of chemical reaction is either accelerated or retarded by the *intervention* of a third substance. (Bengali)
8. The substance which *encourages* or *discourages* the reaction...is called catalyst. (Telugu)

9. The action which is being *done* by the substance is catalysis. (Telugu)
10. At the end manganese dioxide is *left behind.* (Hindi)
11. ...to prevent the reaction to *happen* in the reverse direction.... (Hindi)

In the case of a few sentences, the source of oddness lies within TE. The interference has been from the register of one branch into that of another. One of the sentences produced was, 'the reaction is carried out by enzymes *emitted* by a living body'. In TE, what has been called 'malapropism', is also evidenced. This is quite understandable in view of the fact that TE is full of similar-looking, polysyllabic words. The following may be a case in point:

12. This is either due to *intermittent* compounds or to the exposure of active surface area to the reagents. Writing on Catalysis, the student had, no doubt, intended to use *intermediate.*

The L_1 habits appear to be responsible for numerous grammatical and vocabulary errors. An interesting factor is the Hindi postposition [se] which corresponds to several English prepositions: *by, for, since, from* and *with*. Such distinctions of usage as are expressed by different words in the above group are not made in Hindi, and the postposition [se] covers the whole area. The result is a possibility of confusion and error. The following type of utterances are often met with:

13. *Multiply both the sides with x^4y^4. (Hindi)
14. *In the preparation of O_2 by $KMnO_4$, the MnO_2 acts as a catalyst. (Hindi)

In the case of nouns, countable/mass contrast is productive of errors, wherever the two languages disagree. *Information,* for example, is frequently pluralised as its Hindi equivalent is a countable noun inflected for the plural. But many such formations may be due to analogy rather than L_1 interference.

Other errors noted in the data, assignable to L_t interference, which involve different grammatical points are illustrated by the following sentences:

15. *Its all properties remain. (Hindi)
16. *As suppose there are two reactants.... (Hindi)
17. *So, the positive catalysis helps us to perform the reaction in very few time. (Hindi)

In the last example the error is due to the fact that the Hindi word [ṭhoγa] which corresponds to English *few* can be used with both countable plural and mass nouns as in [ṭ h o γ e s ∂ m ∂ i m ē] 'in a short time' [ṭ h o γ e g h η t ō m ē] 'in a few hours'. Not many examples of mother tongue interference in vocabulary were found. But the following sentence may have been influenced by L_1.

18. Those matters which *forward* or *nonforward* the velocity of chemical reaction are called catalysis. (Hindi)

Here it is possible to argue that the word forward has been selected under the influence of its Hindi equivalent [a g e b ɘ γ a n a] 'to advance'.

In passing, two peculiarities of the Indian context may be mentioned. In the first place, TE is not thought to be as spontaneous as CE and deliberated speech is permissible in technical communication. Secondly, most of our students learn their science subjects at school in the medium of L_1, and later when they are faced with technical expressions in English, they tend to rely on mental translation of L_1, expressions. It is surmised that both these factors make for greater L_1 influence in TE than in CE, but the matter will have to be fully investigated before a definite statement is made.

Note

1. Once an Indian scholar of mathematics complained to this author that his research paper had been spoiled by a teacher of English. Among many unnecessary corrections made by the latter was one in which the well-known mathematical term *transform* had been changed into *transformation*.

Teaching Semantic Distinctions Through Literature

11

The study of meaning is an extremely knotty problem in linguistics. What Lyons remarked in 1968 is, probably, still true: namely, that "no one has yet presented even the outlines of a satisfactory and comprehensive theory of semantics".[1] However, attempts made by scholars like Jerold J. Katz[2] do represent significant advances. But the terminology of semantics is still rather confusing and lacks the uniformity of a standard usage.[3] Although the term "semantic distinctions" occurs in the literature on semantics, the best way for me would be to define the sense in which I have used it. I prefer to avoid controversies like those relating to reference and sense, although I venture to say that a sensible theory of semantics ought to start with the assumption that linguistic units as code (words in our case) do 'refer' to something outside themselves and then proceed to analyse "reference" into various categories and constituents such as objects, ideas, mental states, grammatical roles and conceptual, affective, stylistic, etc., remarking that in the meaning of each unit these are present in different proportions and any one or more of them may dwindle into zero. To take an extreme case, in "sodium chloride", the affective element is zero and in "ah" the conceptual one.

IRAL, XXIII (1985).

Leech has discussed seven types of meaning: conceptual, connotative, social, affective, reflected, collocative and thematic.[4] I find this treatment of meaning satisfactory for the pedagogical purpose in view, but it seems better for reasons implied in the point made above to call these "Constituents" rather than types. In the following pages, I shall use this classification as a general background.

By "semantic distinctions" I mean small differences in terms of constituents and within a single constituent, for example one constituent less or more, or difference of content-coverage within the conceptual or effective constituent. When words are compared in this study, a certain type of normal context is assumed and polysemic considerations are left out for the sake of simplicity. The semantic distinction between "progeny" and "children" is that the latter has an additional connotative element, that between "dear" and "darling" is that the latter has more of affective content. "Probable" differs from "possible" in that it covers a narrower and specifiable area along a certain modal scale. Similarly, semantic distinctions can be formalised within such lexical sets as "skirmish", "fighting", "engagement", "battle", "war", "gentleman", "person", "chap", "fellow", "give", "donate", "sell", "lend", "murmur", "whisper", "speak", "talk", "harangue"; "think", "consider", "decide", "judge". In teaching situations, however, the theoretical concern for formalisation must not be allowed to hinder the instructor from bringing out the nuances of meaning by contextualisation and explanation, which are necessary for a thorough grasp by the learner.

My subject as outlined above excludes consideration of such relations as antonymy and incompatibility, since they represent major differences, although as Lyons has pointed out a technical identification of both involves similarity along one or more dimensions.[5] However, we are here clearly concerned with minimal, not maximal differences, and practical experience shows that learners tend to get confused more with words which have similar meanings than with opposites or incompatibles. They fail to perceive subtle differences in meaning, which may not be of much consequence in broad situational frames, but which positively interfere with a discriminating use of the language at advanced levels.

We are, then, concerned chiefly with synonymic and hyponymic relations. Synonymy again, is a misleading term. Ullmann has quoted scholars and linguists to the effect that there are no true synonyms.[6] He mentions the nine-point illustration of the typical differences between synonyms given by W.E. Collinson, and is quick to add that a closer look at the series reveals further complexity. Particularly interesting is the suggestion to arrange synonyms "into a series where their distinctive meanings and overtones will stand out by contrast, as for instance the various adjectives denoting swiftness: quick, swift, fast, fleet, rapid, speedy".[7]

Two points ought to be mentioned here. If words with overlapping meanings are arranged in a series, something like componential analysis may be useful in bringing out distinctions, between them. Here the teacher has to adopt a tentative approach, setting up relevant semantic features rather than getting lost in the controversies surrounding the so-called atomic concepts. The technical difficulties and theoretical problems facing componential analysis have been pointed out by Lyons,[8] but the general approach can surely lend method and precision to our presentation of semantic distinctions.

Secondly, arrangement of words into a series as exemplified by Ullmann brings us closer to the "field theory" as proposed by J. Trier and developed by his followers. This theory deals with (roughly speaking) paradigmatic relations of words, charting out a conceptual area within a language. "This notion", says Katz, "stripped down to its linguistic essentials", "is that the vocabulary of a language divides into classes of items, each marking off an integrated conceptual domain within which the conceptual space is differentiated into elementary regions whose boundaries delimit and are delimited by the boundaries of others". In his own treatment, Katz has shown how transformational operations on lexical readings can account for semantic fields.[9] However, Katz's approach is far too complex to lend much support to the teacher.

Nevertheless, the field theory in its general form offers an important insight into the mechanism of meaning and has vital significance for the teaching of semantic distinctions. It leads us beyond synonymy, but does not exclude it. It includes both minor differences of meaning as well as major but related contrasts. It also emphasizes the fact that a word can be understood only in relation to other words in a semantic field and that each word is a member of a lexical set.

Distinctions involved in hyponymy are easier to describe; it denotes an inclusion relationship: the meaning of "scarlet" for example is included in that of "red", of "cow" in that of "animal". Yet this alone, although helpful, will not bring out the distinction clearly and the logical relation of class and member also does not take us far. The distinctions between co-hyponyms remain to be dealt with, for co-hyponyms are not synonymous unless two words (which is rare), e.g. one indigenous and the other borrowing have exactly identical relation with the superordinate term. A further difficulty is that superordinate terms are not everywhere available. For example, colour words have no superordinate term in English.[10]

We are now in a position to state some conclusions. Semantic distinctions can be described in terms of constituents of meaning and by reference to neighbouring items in a semantic field. Synonymy and hyponymy include some finer semantic differences between words which may present difficulties for formal description in terms of discreet conceptual units.

There is another aspect of meaning. Meaning is also dependent on the context of situation: words yield their meaning in context. The importance of context has been generally recognised by both linguists and language-teaching specialists. As an English teacher has remarked, "The first point to make in connection with teaching vocabulary is one that most teachers take for granted today: that the meanings of words must be taught in context—not from lists of unrelated words."[11] I wish to distinguish between different kinds of context from the pedagogical point of view. At the primary level we have what I would call "natural context" in which there is no difference between a real situation and the classroom situation. For example, the teacher ready to call the roll, may say to one of the students, "Can you lend me your pen for a few moments?" Thus setting the word "lend" in context. In practice, I have found that the students nearly always make the right response—handing the pen to the teacher—but the right response is more due to the overwhelming nature of the context including gestures than a clear understanding of the meaning. To take another example, the teacher may invite the students to tea and illustrate the actual use of phatic communion and small talk. Obviously, this kind of contextualisation in real life situations is difficult to arrange and has a limited usefulness in vocabulary teaching. The second type may be called "realistic context" which is provided in the class-room itself. This is comparable with what Corder has called "demonstration". "It means presenting a real or simulated scene in which the speaker and hearer play a part and in which the unknown word or expression occurs in the dialogue."[12]

At an advanced level, if the aim is to teach the finer distinctions between words, both these types of contextualisation have limited utility. We need a context which is both precise and powerful in the sense that it makes a unique appeal to the mind of the learner. The third type, I would call "living context". It is at this point that I wish to introduce the role of creative writing. Poetry, drama and fiction provide a rich variety of living contexts. If it is urged that this type of contextualisation is purely imaginary, I would say that imagination plays a major role in language-use, specially higher type of communication and expression. How many times have we not talked about a struggling crew on high seas, or hunters in pursuit of game, etc., etc., while sitting comfortably in an air-conditioned room: language enables us to visualise all sorts of situations.

Literary writing has certain properties which make it eminently suitable as material for the teaching of finer distinctions of meaning. In the first place, in every kind of imaginative writing, one has to pay special attention to words and their meaning. Quirk gives the title "The Intolerable Wrestle with Words" to a chapter devoted to a discussion of literary language.[13] I must here add a word of caution. A creative writer has a Janus-like attitude to words: now he is concerned with bringing out the exact import of a word, now with forcing the word into a new meaning. There are, however, writers like G.B. Shaw and Robert Frost who pursue exactitude in expression. On the whole, a discriminating attention to language is a necessity for the literary writer, since, as Wellek and Warren have pointed out, literature differs from other arts in that its material is language itself.[14] David Daiches[15] has quoted an interesting observation from W.H. Auden's "Squares and Oblongs":

> "Why do you want to write poetry?" If the young man answers: "I have important things to say", then he is not a poet. If he answers: "I like hanging around words listening to what they say," then maybe he is going to be a poet.

Secondly, a creative writer is endowed with a special capacity to imagine contexts which are appealing for a variety of reasons. They are patterned and even the so-called loose ends are carefully planned. They represent interesting or challenging situations. Above all they have a unique force or verve.

Thirdly, literature has a mnemonic quality. It sticks to the mind. The rhythm, sound-pattern, appeal of incident and the striking nature of utterance help the learning of the minor distinctions of meaning, which matter so much in literature.

Let us now turn to the actual use of literary texts in teaching semantic distinctions.

1. Graphic Concretization

The writer brings out the precise meaning of a word in sensuous terms:

> "Ay", he said aloud. There is no translation for this word and perhaps it is just a noise such as a man might

make involuntarily, feeling the nail go through his hands and into the wood.[16]

No dictionary, I think, can express better the semantic nature and central meaning of the word. The teacher's task will be to add similar interjections and bring out the significant distinctions by description and contextualisation. In the following verse, the significant aspects of the meaning of the word "wander" are gathered in a comparison:

I *wandered* lonely as a cloud

(William Wordsworth, "Daffodils")

2. Two or More Words Given in Context

(a) He had told me stories about the catacombs and about Napoleon Bonaparte, and he had explained to me the meaning of the different ceremonies of the Mass and of the different vestments worn by the priest. Sometimes he had amused himself by putting difficult questions to me, asking me what one should do in certain circumstances or whether such and such sins were *mortal or venial* or only *imperfections.*

(James Joyce, "The Sisters")

(b) Penfold: A London *thief, pick pocket, highwayman*—anything he could turn his dishonest hand to....

(W.W. Jacobs and Charles Rock, *The Ghost of Jerry Bundler*)

(c) Most people are heartless about turtles because a turtle's heart will beat for hours after he has been *cut up* and *butchered.*[17]

(d) Catherine: Of course he sends me the news, Sergius is the *hero* of the hour, the *idol* of the regiment.

(G.B. Shaw, *Arms and The Man,* Act I)

The aid which such excerpts from literature give a teacher is to highlight the possibility of difference between lexical items with overlapping or roughly synonymous meaning. The context contains expressive elements, but explanation is to be supplied by the teacher. He has to deal also within contentive difference, for example, between 'thief' and 'pickpocket' and connotative difference between "hero" and "idol".

3. Distinction Implied

Sometimes an implication in the text is present and the teacher has to develop the distinctions. He may have to supply new terms. In such cases a careful attention must be paid to collocation and grammar, e.g. use of modals and sequence of tenses:

(a) It seemed to come at regular intervals, perhaps three times a minute, and her left hand was in almost constant movement: it was not quite a *tremble,* it was a rapid *twirl* as though she wanted to draw your attention to something behind her back.[18]

(b) Skelton made an effort at conversation, but his host was *taciturn,* and they ended the meal in silence that was only broken by Grange when he got up.[19]

(c) The *tuna,* the fishermen called all the fish of that species tuna and only distinguished among them by their proper names when they came to sell them or to trade them for baits, were down again.[20]

(d) He ate the other part of the piece that he cut in two. He *chewed* it carefully and then *spat* out the skin.[21]

(e) I went to sleep before I went to bed;
Especially in winter when the bed
Might just as well be *ice,* and clothes *snow,*

(Robert Frost, "The Witch of Coos")

4. Meaning Embedded

A creative writer seldom states the meaning of a word as a dictionary or a teacher would. But his method is very effective. He may contextualize the word and explain it in terms of other words distinctively or attempt to demarcate it from them.

(a) Norman Grange was a rubber planter. He was up before daybreak to take roll call of his labour and then walked over the estate to see that the taping was properly done. This duty performed, he came home, bathed and changed, and now with his wife opposite him he was eating the substantial *meal,* half *breakfast* and half *luncheon,* which in Borneo is called *brunch.*[22]

(b) Paul.

You are the universal *fugitive—*
Escapist as we say—though you are not
Running away from Him you think you are,

(Robert Frost, *A Masque of Mercy*)

5. Semantic Held Covered

In drama and fiction wider contexts are dealt with more fully than in poetry, short stories and one-act plays and the latter have the advantage of elaborating on a detail. The former provide rich material for the teaching of a series of words loosely covering a semantic field. The changing pattern of context is vitally supportive to the distinctions of meaning. I must clarify a relevant point here. The terms in a semantic field are not always in strictly paradigmatic relation: they are distributed, as it were, within a three-dimensional conceptual space, lying over and against one another. Where two lexical items are in strict choice-relation, we cannot use them syntagmatically, e.g. "red" and "yellow". But it is important to note that, although in one sense we cannot say, "he was a good captain and soldier", in another, we can, and in the latter sense, a semantic distinction is clearly intended. This is so because word-series can be constructed along any of a number of dimensions, e.g. leadership, fighting. In my discussion, wherever I deal with word-series, I have in the background some sort of semantic field including affective and other components of meaning and not only the conceptual one, but evidently my main aim is not to propose methods for the teaching of semantic fields as such.

To return to the subject under discussion, a scene in a play or a section in a novel is based on some area of experience, including states of the mind. In semantic terms, the writer gives expression to this context by employing clusters of words representing different divisions which roughly correspond to fields. It is possible to isolate these clusters and deal with the semantic distinctions present.

Let us consider an example. There is an interesting presentation of a semantic field connected with the expression of displeasure in various forms and degrees in Act I of *Arms and The Man* by G.B. Shaw. Raina confronted with Bluntschli is staggered by his lack of soldierly qualities and by what appears to her meanness and cowardice. In his stage directions, Shaw indicates Raina's reactions to the variations of Bluntschli's unworthiness. He uses a series of words, all of which connote displeasure, but they differ in minor but significant respects from one another and the context offers a clue to the semantic distinctions between them. The series consists of the following expressions:

disdainfully
(cutting him short)
(with dignified patience)
revolted
superciliously
outraged
scornfully
loftily
ironically
sternly
Coldly

The words of course do not appear in a regular scale of ascending intensity, since the fluctuations of life situations are not as patterned as theoretical constructs, but they all share the central meaning of denunciatory attitude. The teacher can rearrange them in pattern and with the help of context so well provided by the playwright bring out the distinctions in meaning in terms of constituents, e.g., stern = displeasure + strictness; cold = displeasure + unfriendly. He can also fill the gaps by introducing some missing terms like "angrily", "furiously", "sarcastically".

Some minor series are also present in the First Act.

(a) Elation (Raina's reactions to the news of victory)
eagerly
with a cry of delight (delightedly)
rapturously
ecstatically
frantically (kiss one another...)
with surging enthusiasm (enthusiastically)
excitedly

(b) Subdual (Bluntschli's calculated moves to silence Raina)
threateningly
warning(ly)
commandingly
menacingly
formidably.

The example is also intended to show how a semantically oriented analysis of literary texts can be useful in isolating and fabricating suitable material for the teaching of semantic distinctions. Not all authors are equally eligible for this purpose. I do not wish to enter into the question of suitability further. Suffice it to say that a concern for word meaning and some respect for rationality and ordinary language would be desirable qualifications in an author.

I would like to conclude this discussion with two considerable implications for materials-production. The use of certain grammatical criteria in selection and grading of reading texts is now fairly common. Vocabulary selection, too, as pointed out by Mackey, has an old history.[23] Most of the work, however, is in the areas of frequency-count as regards meanings and degrees of difficulty. Wilkins has pointed out that "a study of the different synonyms, antonyms and hyponyms that a word has may well be the only way that the full meaningfulness of a word can be brought out".[24] Material has been produced on these lines also. What is needed in selection and grading of material is, *inter alia*, consideration of semantic distinctions, which are of vital importance in comprehension and expression. I have demonstrated the value of literary texts for this purpose. Since semantic distinctions are relevant at higher stages when the students' motivation can be maintained only by challenging material capable of affording a superior kind of interest, literature, rather widely defined, is the only choice. I leave die specific procedure of selection and presentation for a future date.

Secondly, lexicography is also affected by my proposal. Samuel Johnson was the first dictionary-maker who recognised the value of citations. "His use of illustrative quotations", says Thomas Pyles, "literally by the thousands, was an innovation".[25] As Halliday has pointed out, the technique of definition has clear limitations and citations are required to bring out the collocational relations of a word.[26] Modern pedagogical dictionaries do make use of citations from ordinary language. This method is quite useful for ordinary purposes. But if we recognise semantic distinctions as a separate problem in the teaching of meaning, a different technique is called for. This will require the use of suitable citations from literature. Such citations, as I have illustrated will take care of synonyms and hyponyms much better than the mere listing of items in dictionaries with supposedly identical meaning. Literary citations have the additional advantage of being memorable and quotable.

References

1. John Lyons, *Introduction to Theoretical Linguistics* (London: Cambridge Univ. Press, 1968), 402.
2. Jerrold J. Katz, *Semantic Theory* (New York: Harper & Row, 1972).
3. John Lyons, *op. cit.*, 403.
4. G.N. Leech, *Semantics* 2nd. ed. (Harmondsworth: Penguin, 1981), 9-23.
5. John Lyons, *Semantics I* (London: Cambridge Univ. Press, 1977), 270-90.
6. Stephen Ullmann, *Semantics: An Introduction to the Science or Meaning* (Oxford : Basil Blackwell, 1972), 141.
7. *Ibid.*, 142-44.
8. John Lyons, *Semantics I*, 317-35.
9. Jerrold Katz, *op. cit.*, 346-55.
10. John Lyons, *Introduction to Theoretical Linguistics*, 456.

11. Paul Nation, "Techniques for Teaching Vocabulary" in *English Teaching Forum* XII, 3 (July-September, 1974), 18.
12. S. Pit Corder, "The Teaching of Meaning" in *Applied Linguistics and the Teaching of English,* 2nd. ed., ed. by H. Fraser and W.R. O'Donnell (London : ELBS 1973), 156.
13. Randolph Quirk, *The Use of English,* 2nd ed. (London: ELBS, 1972), 262.
14. Rene Wellek and Austin Warren, *Theory of Literature,* 3rd ed. (Harmondsworth: Penguin, 1966), 22.
15. David Daiches, *Critical Approaches to Literature* (New Delhi: Orient Longman, 1977), 159.
16. Ernest Hemingway, *The Old Man and the Sea* (New York: Bantam Books, 1965), 98-99.
17. *Ibid.*, 28.
18. Somerset Maugham, "Flotsam and Jetsam" in *Collected Short Stories,* Vol. 2 (London: Pan Books, 1975), 77.
19. *Ibid.*, 89.
20. Ernest Hemingway, *op. cit.,* 32.
21. *Ibid.*, 50.
22. Somerset Maugham, "Flotsam and Jetsam", *op. cit.,* 72.
23. W.F. Mackey, *Language Teaching Analysis* (London: Longman, 1965), 195.
24. D.A. Wilkins, *Linguistics in Language Teaching* (London: Edward Arnold, 1972), 131-32.
25. Thomas Pyles, *The Origin & Development of the English Language,* 2nd ed. (New York: Harcourt Brace Jovanovich, 1971), 224.
26. Angus McIntosh and M.A.K. Halliday, *Patterns of Language: Papers in General, Descriptive and Applied Linguistics* (London: Longman, 1966), 18-19.

Teaching Materials in Technical English

12

In preparing teaching materials in a language, it is necessary, first of all to have a clear idea about the goals, not only the kinds of skill and ability sought to be developed in the pupil, but also the variety of register of the language in which proficiency is desired. It will be a grave error to proceed with the task of materials production in Technical English (TE) as if it were not much different from the other varieties of English or from Common English (CE).

Before any teaching materials—textbooks, grammar books or exercises—illustrative of the special features of TE, can be produced, we must carefully notice the characteristics of TE and the way it is distinct from CE. Although the general linguistic structure is the same in all varieties of English, TE has certain distinctive phonological, morphological, syntatic and semantic features and certain aspects of the structure assume greater importance in it than others. A.J. Herbert states that 'the language in which scientific and technical facts are expressed is certainly not a different language from that of everyday life, but all the same it presents the foreign students with a number of special problems.[1] But the material found in Kelly would suggest that the native speaker too has to make a conscious effort for the mastery of Technical English.[2]

Indian Journal of Applied Linguistics, Vol. 1, No. 2, 1975.

Generally speaking technical language is a form of language used for the expression of specialised knowledge pertaining to nature and conditions of life. It seeks to present facts in a series of objective, direct, and unambiguous statements. All technical expression follows certain broad principles, irrespective of the subject matter expressed, but in the present discussion we will use the term 'technical English' for the register employed in the 'texts' of science and technology.

Technical English has the following special features:

(i) **Phonology:** There are hundreds of unfamiliar forms composed of Greek and Latin elements whose polysyllabic structures require special attention. The Indian student tends to mispronounce even short forms such as *fungi, scyphozoa* and *xylene.* Then there are numerous names of scientists from all over the world with peculiar sound patterns. Next, many obvious features of conversational English such as contracted forms are not commonly found in TE. Lastly the objective attitude of the statement requires only a partial use of the complex intonational scale of English.

(ii) **Grammar**: TE morphology includes some additional processes. In CE compounds are formed by putting two or more free morphemes together with certain phonological changes and the meaning of the new word can be gathered from the component parts as in *air-raid, top-most* and *sky-blue.* In TE the favourite method of compounding is the coalescing of two or more Greek or Latin elements into a single word as in *protoplasm, isotope* and *epidiascope.* Word-formation by conversion of proper nouns is quite common as in *newton, ohm, watt.* The second peculiarity of TE morphology is 'irregular plurals' and adjectives like *focus: foci; amoeba: amoebae; analysis: analyses; focus: focal; formula: formulaic.* A great majority of technical terms are derived from Greek and Latin and they continue to form their plurals and adjectives according to the rules of their parent languages. Among the chief syntactic features of TE are the use of neutral present, passive construction without agentive phrase, conditional clause and a general lack of those patterns which are common in familiar dialogue, e.g. question tags and exclamations.

(iii) **Semantics**: The semantic 'sets' and 'fields' of TE are well marked and distinct from those of CE. Familiar words such as *force, work, power* and *mixture* have 'defined' meanings. Ambiguity has no ambiguity in TE, for it has its original meaning, 'going in both ways', as in the 'ambiguous case' where two triangles can be drawn from the same data.

The most obvious characteristic of TE is technical vocabulary. Each branch of science and technology has its own jargon which makes it nearly unintelligible to the common user of English and strongly sets it apart from the other registers.

Style is of great significance in TE. The 'Impersonal style' which is proper to TE is formal, objective and descriptive. It is achieved by the use of descriptive terms, set phrases, functional use of pronouns *we* and *you* and what has been called 'impersonal passive'. Lastly it must be noted that mathematics is an integral part of the communication system of TE and a genuine piece of technical writing cannot exclude it completely.

It is essential to grasp the structure of TE for the production of teaching materials, but not enough, for we must also take into account the recent ideas on language teaching in general. "Judging from techniques and trends of the past few years, we can see that current thinking in methodology seems to be in the direction of: (a) relaxation of some of the more extreme restrictions of the audiolingual method, and (b) development of techniques requiring a more active use of the students' mental powers."[3] It is no longer insisted that speech training is the soul of language teaching; reading and writing, specially for an advanced course or a specialised one like TE, are treated as equally important and an integrated approach to language teaching as regards the four skills, is being developed. It is felt that successful language activity demands proficiency in all the skills and it is unrealistic to separate them widely or give priority to listening and speaking at the cost of reading and writing. Similarly, a judicious use of the mother tongue is considered not only permissible but also beneficial. "Notable among current trends is a more practical recognition of the varying needs of students. If, for instance, a student needs a reading knowledge of English above all else, then reading must have first priority, and the student must learn that skill through specific guided practice in reading."[4]

Speech may be regarded as primary in a sense. But, as Sharwood Smith has said, "in certain teaching situations speech is definitely secondary—for example, in courses for students whose first need is to read and write the target language".[5] Dealing with the basic principles in teaching writing, he further suggests that the teaching of written language has to be viewed both as a language problem and as a rhetorical or stylistic problem and discusses at some length the well established principle of controlled or guided writing.[6]

Language learning is no longer viewed as a mechanical process of habit formation; Chomskyan theories have proved it to be a creative activity. No teaching material can, therefore, be scientific and beneficial unless it secures the mental involvement of the learner by arousing his interest and curiosity.

We are now in possession of the requisite theoretical background in the light of which the governing considerations for the production of teaching materials in TE may be set up.

To begin with, the main teaching material must be a genuine piece of TE with the typical structure saliently entrenched for the teaching strategy of the instructor. It is not enough for the material to be concerned with a scientific or technical subject, it must follow the rules of the game. It is therefore vital that the material be chosen from scientific writing proper, including textbooks on science and technology, or if the material is composed for specific purposes, it must conform to the norms. It must offer enough of linguistic material for discussion and exercise. I have found the passages in A.J. Herbert's *The Structure, of Technical English* (1965) admirably fulfilling this requirement although the material is deficient on another count to be discussed later. *A Preparatory General English Course for College* (physical science) only partially meets the requirement.[7] R.A. Kelly's book, *The Use of English for Technical Students* (1962) adequately offers genuine samples of TE. He unequivocally states his case in the Preface: "I make no apology for the absence of 'literary' type of exercise. While I realise quite well that engineers are human, that they enjoy literature and are not blind to the beauties of our language. I also realise how great is their need for a guide to exposition—something to help them to escape from that hybrid literary scientific writing which they often bring with them to a technical course."

The question is whether popular science writing and science fiction can be considered fit material for teaching TE. Strictly speaking the answer must be, No. Books like *Physics for the Modern World* by E.N. Da C. Andarde, *Chemistry for the Modern World* by George Porter, *Simple Science* by E.N. Da C. Andarde and Julian Huxley, *Introducing Science* by Alan Isaacs, and the delightful popular science writing of George Gamon are quite informative and occasionally go very deep into the subject, but their chief intention is to acquaint the layman with scientific and technical things in the language and style he can appreciate. In their attempt the authors necessarily simplify the subject-matter and in the process relieve it of its mathematical component and often sacrifice accuracy. Their writing is diluted for the consumption of the common reader whereas strictly 'technical' writing is intended for a specialist.

But as ancillary reading and as raw material for exercises, popular science writing is eminently suited for certain purposes. It may be used to highlight by contrast the salient linguistic and stylistic features of TE. Popular science writing being explanatory and periphrastic is ideal for elementary exercises in precis-writing. In the course of precis-making the student practices the use of technical terms and economy of expression. We may also frame questions of the following type:

(i) Given below is a passage of popular science writing. Try to make it more technical by appropriately introducing technical terms and mathematical expressions.

(ii) Replace the italicized portions by suitable technical terms.

(iii) Rewrite the following passage in impersonal style.

Science fiction is on a different footing. It is a genre of literature and its primary aim is to entertain the reader and afford him aesthetic pleasure. It is never a matter-of-fact description of the scientific theory and seldom deals with cold facts in an objective way. It explores the possibilities of man's use of science and technology and throws the gold-dust of imagination on ordinary objects. Again, we cannot employ science fiction as proper material for TE but it is not without use. It can always be used for rapid reading and comprehension questions which take the learner into the field of technical language. Jules Verne in *Twenty Thousand Leagues Under the Sea* describes the Nautilus with much scientific ingenuity. When we ask the pupil to state the scientific principle on which the working of the submarine is based we are leading him into technical composition.

Another source of fascinating reading is provided by books on the history of science and the biographies of scientists. Books like, *Science and its Background* by H.D. Anthony; *Science: Past and Present* by P. Sherwood Taylor; *Science in the Middle Ages* by A.C. Crombie; *Great Scientists,* by Thomas and Thomas; 100 *Great Scientists,* edited by Jay E. Greene, are highly entertaining but they cannot be adopted as teaching material in TE. Like science fiction, they may be used for general reading or selectively and adaptively for specific purposes.

We said earlier that the modern methodology of language teaching insists on an integrated approach and it is also conceded that in some situations, where the needs of the learner demand, reading and writing may receive priority over speech training. In our situation reading comprehension and technical composition are of prime importance for the student of science and technology. Our teaching materials must therefore be suitable for practising spelling, punctuation, paragraph structure and linking as well as different forms of exposition, e.g. description, explanation, report writing and the proper style.

Lastly, we must consider the problem of securing the learner's interest and mental involvement and examine specific teaching material from an overall viewpoint. It is not enough for the teaching material to be on a scientific or technical subject and possess the structure of technical language. It must offer a thematic and linguistic challenge to the learner; it must arouse his curiosity and absorb his intellect. [We will explain the point by reference to *A Preparatory General Course for Colleges* (Physical Sciences) and A.J. Herbert's *The Structure of Technical English*.]

A Preparatory General English Course, contains reading passages on such topics as pressure, gravity, elements, electricity and bacteria with a good deal of language work in Part II. Most of the passages are composed in a long-winded hybrid, school-teaching style with loss of accuracy and significant detail in many cases; there is very little in them to engage the mind of a boy who has passed the High School with Science and there is much in the condescending tone which may annoy him. For whatever the material may be useful, it militates against the basic canons of Technical English and cannot be used for teaching it. The following extract from Gravity will make the point clear:

> When you throw a ball up, it goes slower until the critical moment when the force moving it up is exactly equal in magnitude to the force (called the force of gravity) pulling it down; for a moment the ball is stationary; then it begins to move in the opposite direction, downwards. If two balls of different weight begin to fall simultaneously (at the same time), they descend at the same speed and reach your hands, or the ground, simultaneously. In a vacuum, a vessel with all the air removed—a feather and a piece of metal fall side by side, your physics lecturer will probably show you this. If you can, put a small piece of thin paper on top of a 50 nP coin (the paper should not project past the rim of the coin), hold the coin horizontally and then release it; you will see that the paper falls with the same velocity as the coin.
>
> When a cricket ball is in the air, if we want to be completely accurate we must say that the cricket ball

> and the earth are pulling each other, but the earth is such a large sphere and the ball is so minute by comparison that we can ignore the attraction of the earth by the ball; it is negligible in magnitude. It is because of the negligible mass of falling objects by comparison with the earth that they fall at the same rate. The moon is about 1/50 the size of the earth, and when we speak of the moon revolving round the earth, this is not quite accurate. The earth is drawn towards the moon, too, and both revolve around a centre, which, however, is still beneath the surface of the earth. We see the force which the moon exerts on the earth twice each day when the water of the oceans moves about 40 cms. towards the moon.
>
> Sir Isaac Newton gave the 'law of gravitation' as an explanation for the behaviour of things on the earth and in the universe. This law states that every particle in the universe attracts every other particle with a force which is inversely proportional to the square of the distance between them (Don't worry about this now).

It is almost certain that the student we have in mind will no more get such material in his normal reading and will never be expected to write such things—not even as a popularizer of science, for popular science writing is vastly more interesting and powerful. On the contrary if he develops this style, it is going to be a permanent handicap in his future career. How different from this is technical English is obvious from the following extract from *Physics,* Pt. I by Resnick and Halliday:

> One of the forces encountered is rigid body motions in the force of gravity. Actually this is not just one force but the resultant of a great many forces. Each particle in the body is acted on by a gravitational force. If the body of mass M is imagined to be divided into a large number of particles, say n, the gravitational force exerted by the earth on i-th particle of mass mi is mig. This force is directed down towards the earth. If the acceleration due to gravity g is the same everywhere in a region, we say that a uniform gravitational field

> exists there; that is g has the same magnitude and direction everywhere in that region. For a rigid body in a uniform gravitational field, g must be the same for each particle in the body and the weight forces on the particles must be parallel to one another.

The passages given in A.J. Herbert are much better in that more or less they may pass as specimens of technical writing and they display the structure of TE in nearly all its essentials except for the fact that a scrupulous omission of the mathematical component gives them a slightly odd look. The material offers rich resources for practice and exercise. We take the following example in which the schematic diagram of a blast furnace could not be included:

> The earth contains a large number of metals which are useful to man. One of the most important of these is iron. Modern industry needs considerable quantities of this metal, either in the form of iron or in the form of steel. A certain number of non-ferrous metals, including aluminium and zinc, are also important but even today the majority of our engineering products are of iron or steel. Moreover, iron possesses magnetic properties, which have made die development of electrical power possible.
>
> The iron ore which we find in the earth is not pure. It contains some impurities which we must remove by smelting. The process of smelting consists of heating the ore in a blast furnace with coke and limestone, and reducing it to metal. Blasts of hot air enter the furnace from the bottom and provide the oxygen which is necessary for the reduction of the ore. The ore becomes molten and its oxides combine with carbon from the coke. The non-metallic constituents of the ore combine with the limestone to form a liquid slag. This floats on top of the molten iron, and passes out of the furnace through a tap. The metal which remains is pig-iron.
>
> We can melt this down again in another furnace—a cupola—with more coke and limestone, and tap it out into a ladle or directly into moulds. This is *cast-iron.*

> Cast-iron does not have the strength of steel. It is brittle and may fracture under tension. But it possesses certain properties which make it very useful in the manufacture of machinery. In the molten state it is very fluid, and therefore it is easy to cast it into intricate shapes. Also it is easy to machine it. Cast-iron contains small proportions of other substances. These non-metallic constituents of cast-iron include carbon, silicon and sulphur, and the presence of these substances affects the behaviour of the metal. Iron which contains a negligible quantity of carbon, for example, *wrougbt-iron,* behaves differently from iron which contains a lot of carbon.
>
> The carbon in cast-iron is present partly as free graphite and partly as a chemical combination of iron and carbon which we call cementite. This is a very hard substance, and it makes the iron hard too. However, iron can only hold about 1½% of cementite. Any carbon content above the percentage is present in the form of a flaky graphite. Steel contains no free graphite, and its carbon content ranges from almost nothing to 1½%. We make wire and tubing from mild steel with a very low carbon content, and drills and cutting tools from high carbon steel.

It will be interesting to compare the above with a similar extract from a textbook, *College Chemistry* by Keenan and Wood.

> *Open Hearth Process of Making Steel.* Open Hearth Process of Making Steel has largely displaced the Bessemer process; it now accounts for about 90 per cent of the steel produced in this country. The average hearth is a shallow vessel, 40 by 18 ft. and 2 ft. deep. Over it is a roof of arched fire brick against which hot fuel gases are burned. The materials charged into the hearth are pig iron, rusty scrap iron (Fe_2O_3 on the surface) or smaller amounts of iron ore, and other materials for special alloys.

The hearth is lined with either a basic or an acidic lining, depending on the type of pig iron being purified. In this country the ores usually have acid impurities (phosphorus or sulfur), so basic linings such as magnesium and calcium oxide are used. When the charge of 100 or more tons is melted in the hearth, the iron rust (or iron ore) may take part in the following typical reactions:

$2Fe_2O_3 + 3S \longrightarrow 4Fe + 3SO_2$

$2Fe_2O_3 + 3C \longrightarrow 4Fe + 3CO_2$

$1OFe_2O_3 + 12P \longrightarrow 20Fe + 3P_4O_{10}$

The Co_2 gas bubbles out of the melt, and the sulfur and phosphorous oxides combine with basic oxides of the lining to form a slag.

The process is slow enough (about eight hours) so that chemical analyses can be made periodically to check the composition of the steel. This greater control of composition is perhaps the chief advantages of the open hearth process over the Bessemer.

But little in the kind of reading material we find in A.J. Herbert can arouse the learner's curiosity or hold his mind. He has dealt with commonplaces of science and technology which most pupils will consider too familiar to need any attention.

From what I have said about the two textbooks above. It should not be concluded that they are of no use at all, far from that, they represent pioneering work in a field not fully covered so far and contain goods practice material for science and technology students. But we can hardly fully approve of materials which do little to secure the mental involvement of the learner. The question here is that of choosing the right kind of topics from the technical texts. Recent advances for example are sure to engage the attention of the learner rather than hackneyed subjects; scientific explanations of familiar phenomena e.g. the physico-chemical processes involved in washing of clothes with soap, may be quite interesting, and so may be technical texts with a speculative touch (not science fiction, of course) e.g. speculative writing about the 'heat death' of the universe. Then there are old topics not yet exhausted, for example the atom has not yet yielded all its secrets and a passage on the structure of the atom may still be quite engaging.

Since for the achievement of our main goals we must remain within the technical register, a direct source of reading material is the textbook of science and technology provided we fish for the right kind of material with care and diligence. One will have to wade through hundreds of pages before one comes to what may be called a 'purple passage' in technical writing. For the purpose, one has to consult the best writers of technical texts and one such writer is superior to another by, among other things, the degree to which he can hold the mind of the reader. George Gamow, Linus Pauling, C.W. Keenan and J.H. Wood, R. Resnick and D. Halliday, Carl P. Swanson and A.J. Mee have been found quite useful from this point of view.

Once a suitable passage has been selected, language work starts. Ignoring the details of technique, we must mention a point which must be the governing principle in framing exercises. We are dealing here with students who are no longer school-boys and have already done a course in English and therefore the questions we ask, the exercises and tests we give, must be of a challenging nature. I do not wish to elaborate the point further beyond giving a few short specimens which in my view are challenging.

1. Spot and explain the grammatical error in each of the following sentences:
   - (a) Each of these two forms of energy contribute to the mass which is a characteristic property of matter.
   - (b) We find no difficulty to move through the air.
   - (c) Placed between the legs of the Vernier Callipers, we can measure the dimensions of a body.
   - (d) The velocities of gas molecules often exceed a riffle bullet.
   - (e) The movement of a star through space, relative to the earth, can be observed through a telescope

provided that the star is not moving directly away or towards the earth.

2. In the following passage use appropriate forms of the verbs indicated within brackets:

   A living cell, however (be) always more fascinating than a dead one. (Watch) cells (divide) (be) (witness) one of the most dramatic of biological phenomena. The phase-contrast microscope (permit) the cytologist (do) this.

3. Improve the following sentences which lack coherence, unity, or clarity:
   (a) Here is a piece of paper to draw the curve.
   (b) It is desirable to however revise the principles involved.
   (c) To do this we must find the temperature of 30° on the horizontal axis and a perpendicular is plotted from that point until it intersects the solubility curve.

4. Write separately the topic sentence of each paragraph and underline the linking portions.

5. Analyse the following terms:
   tribology, amphibious, trigonometry.

6. Rewrite the following sentences in impersonal style:
   (a) Cancer is a terrifying disease.
   (b) When I heat a lump of calcium I see it burn with a brick-red flame.

7. Fill in the blanks with suitable words in the following descriptions: an ammeter is an instrument for measuring the...of an...in....

There is an aspect of materials production in language teaching which we have reserved for special mention: it refers to considerations of a contrastive nature. We have noted what may be called 'double interference phenomena' in the technical English of Indian students, that is, an interference from both L_1 and Common English. Examples are:

(a) Multiply both the sides with x^4y^4.

(b) In Chemistry we define catalysis as a process by which the rate of chemical reaction is either accelerated or retarded by the intervention of a third substance.

In (a) above the error represents interference from L_1 and in (b) from Common English.

Such interference is attested at all levels—phonology grammar and semantics.

It is to be concluded, therefore, that a comparison of TE structure with those of CE and L_1, in carefully selected items, where differences are quite marked, may reveal areas of difficulty and thus be a factor in the selection and processing of teaching materials in Technical English.

References

1. Herbert, A.J. (1965). *The Structure of Technical English* (ELBS).
2. Kelly, R.A. (1965). *The Use of English For Technical Students* (ELBS).
3. "Current Trends in Language Teaching", A Forum Staff Article, *English Teaching Forum*, Vol. I, January-March 1974.
4. *Ibid.*
5. Sharwood Smith, M.A., July-Sept., 1974. "Teaching Written English: Problems and Principles". *English Teaching Forum*, Vol. XII, 3.
6. *Ibid.*
7. *A Preparatory General English Course for Colleges* (Physical Sciences, Central Institute of English), Orient Longmans, 1963.

Dialogue and Dialogue Teaching

13

Nearly every book on the teaching of English includes dialogue. Most of them present dialogue as a means of inculcating basic language skills and vocabulary, not as an end in itself, as a form of discourse employed in social interaction by the members of a speech community. Lado (1977: 61-69) describes the value of memorizing dialogues as against isolated sentences; dialogues present sentences in context, and they can be dramatized. But Lado looks upon dialogue as a useful tool for teaching language—that is, pronunciation, grammar and vocabulary. Although he mentions the need for cultural notes in a general way, he does not go into detail nor does he say anything about dialogue as discourse or about culturally determined behaviour patterns accompanying, sometimes replacing, the verbal output. According to Bennett (1968: 81), "the teacher's function in the 'conversation', or as it is sometimes more honestly called, 'display' session, is to furnish visual or situational material which will allow the class to reproduce in various combinations, already known units of the target language". Talking about material, Bennett (1968: 133) says that a full-scale general course would feature among other things "familiarity with social aspects of the life of the speech community". Bright and McGregor (1978: 191) include dialogue, along with debate, recitation and play acting, as an item in the teaching of speech. They mention the practice of

English Teaching Forum, Vol. XXV, No. 1, January 1987.

some teachers, who "begin with dialogue, home-made plays and play-reading and demand maximum comprehensibility and phonological behaviour that goes with it for the sake of the success of the play".

Socio-linguistic Aspects of Dialogue

The focus in all the books I have referred to is on language, and the discoursal and other socio-linguistic aspects of dialogue are mentioned either in passing or not at all. The purpose of my comments is not to criticize the authors of these books, but rather to show the overwhelming trend in the treatment of dialogue in books on language teaching. After all, dialogue is a very useful means in language teaching, but it must be realized that teaching language skills with the help of dialogue is not dialogue teaching. Newmark and Diller (1978: 98-101), in their article "Emphasizing the Audio in the Audio-lingual Approach", discuss what they calls the dialogue-pattern-drill approach. They are also working within the old framework of linguistic and learning theory, but in the steps they outline for the teacher, such as role-playing and "free (but guided) conversation closely paralleling the situations in the dialogues," they show a wider awareness. This, however, cannot be regarded as a breakthrough.

My purpose is to bring new socio-linguistic insights to bear on the definition and teaching of dialogue. The insights themselves are not new, but they have not yet found a place in the theory and practice of language instruction. I became aware of the new dimensions of the subject while supervising a research project of Sahab Abdul Aziz Salih (1983), who has explored the topic in some depth and presented a new method for the teaching of dialogue.[1] Discourse analysis is of a special relevance to the study of dialogue, and I shall draw on the contributions of workers in that field, although as will be seen, purely scientific descriptions cannot be adopted in pedagogy without modification and simplification to suit practical needs and limitations.

One major difficulty in discourse analysis is the terminology, which is far from standardized, so that terms are not always used to mean exactly the same thing. The word *discourse* itself has been variously used. Criper and Widdowson (1975: 200), acknowledging the confusion, adopt "the relations between sentences and social meanings and actions" as their definition of *discourse.* I would, however, propose that when a piece of language is viewed as a pattern of "linguistic behaviour" based in social conventions, it is called discourse. Dialogue is a kind of discourse in which two persons talk face to face, with a view to maintaining personal equation and social solidarity.

Culturally Determined Phenomena

I would like to elaborate some important implications of the above view of dialogue. As discourse, dialogue is patterned behaviour, the pattern being determined culturally. When two persons meet, who is to make the first move in greeting? In our society, if the participants are from the same social stratum, the younger in age is expected to make the first move; if they have difference in status, then it is the one who occupies a lower place. In Iraq (and this, I guess, is true of the whole Arab culture), the one occupying a higher position begins first. In Arab culture, after greeting a person, you inquire about his health; in India, about the well-being of his children. In England, apart from the formulaic "how are you?" you comment on the weather. While in Iraq, I was often confronted with the question, "How's your health, doctor?" Some cultures are intolerant of interruptions; ours doesn't take them so seriously. In some cultures the first move in greeting is frequently nonverbal—a smile, or some kind of gesture; in others it is a formulaic expression accompanied by some gesture or facial expression.

This brings us to the ethnography of dialogue. Of all forms of discourse, dialogue is most closely linked with the system of gestures each culture has, and audio-visual recordings of natural dialogue clearly indicate the significance of gestures. Quite often in dialogue the verbal behaviour is punctuated with gesture signs that express assent, disapproval, negation, irritation, indifference, or contempt. A nod, a shake of the head, a shrugging of the shoulders, or a grimace may take the place of a verbal response, and the dialogue will proceed as if something has been said. Now, gestures are by no means universal. Within India itself a nod and a shake are differently gesticulated in the North and the South. A nod in the South is very similar to the shake of a head in the North, and this causes misunderstanding. Shrugging the shoulders is very common in England, and one must know the meaning of this signal. This aspect of dialogue is of considerable importance, particularly when one's aim is to prepare learners for natural dialogue beyond mere mimicry in the classroom. "If the language teacher wishes to develop in his pupils an ability to use the system of the language appropriately as a means of social interaction with native speakers, he will have to be aware of just how the system is used and how its use relates to other forms of communication (Criper and Widdowson 1975: 162). To gestures may be added such other phenomena as facial expressions, eye contact, finger movements, and posture. These non-verbal signs form an integral part of natural conversation. A systematic discussion of this subject can be found in John Goslling's article "Kinesics in Discourse" (1981: 158-84). He has quoted an ailluminating remark by Abercrombie: "We speak with our vocal organs, but we converse without entire bodies; conversation consists of much more than a simple interchange of spoken words." Gosling's description is based on analyzed data, and he finds justification for the creation of a new level of kinesics in discourse analysis.

Other Phenomena of Natural Dialogue

In addition to interjections, we have a class of vocal sounds that occur frequently in natural dialogue: *mm*, *er*, *uhuh*, and silences or zero responses of various kinds. These phenomena used to be ignored and discouraged. But it can now be demonstrated that they are highly meaningful and represent a mode of adjustment to the social and psychological exigencies of conversation. Natural dialogue is not planned or prepared beforehand: you may be confronted with all kinds of questions or remarks—even embarrassing ones, and those that require quick reflection, or to which you wish to react with caution, circumspection, reservation, or hesitation. The phenomena mentioned above enable us to meet this situation successfully. But again, they are by no means universal: each culture has its own non-linguistic vocal signs to express reservation and hesitation, etc. Such vocal sounds are often omitted in a transcription, causing much loss to the tissue of living speech.

A little above these in the linguistic structure are set expressions such as *I think, you know, you see, you know what I mean, so to say, well,* and *O.K.* These devices perform a variety of functions: they give us time to improvise a response, to implicate the co-participant in a delicate matter, to draw attention to something, to lay emphasis, etc. Thus, far from being superfluous, these forms have a practical utility and represent a significant part of linguistic behaviour.

Lastly, we have a special use of grammatical structure in dialogue. In natural conversation, we take several liberties with grammar and logic: sentences may be left incomplete, or the co-participant may be allowed to complete a sentence, parts of sentences may be repeated, single words and phrases are freely made to stand for sentences, speech acts are performed in a variety of sentence patterns or by non-linguistic means. A question may be asked by means of a gesture, a single word, or statement pattern with, of course, the appropriate intonation.

Intonation itself as employed in dialogue is a highly complex phenomenon. In a dialogue, where single phrases or words are frequently used, intonation has 'an enhanced function of indicating the speech acts and the intentions of the speaker. It provides a key to the attitude and reaction of the participants. Its wider functions are involved in the structure of discourse, and many structural distinctions are entirely dependent on intonation. The inevitable conclusion of this brief discussion is that intonation plays a far richer role in dialogue than in many other forms of discourse e.g., prepared lectures, discussion, and even debate.

Analyzing Discourse

We may now turn to the analysis of discourse. Discourse analysis took a wrong turn at its very inception. The first important model was presented in 1975 by Sinclair and

Coulthard (1975). The analytical was categories created on the analogy of earlier Hallidyan framework represent a pioneering effort, not yet superseded by any better proposal. But the Sinclair-Coulthard model arose from a study of teacher-pupil interaction—that is, a specific situation. Subsequent work has faced considerable problems in fitting this model to general data, namely, natural conversation. Moreover, empirically, it was a wrong start: proceeding from a particular to a general theory. The evolution of modern linguistic theory took an opposite direction. The pioneers, Saussure and Bloomfield, built the framework on an examination of the common variety of language, and it was much later in the development of the theory that modified models for specific varieties of the language, such as technical language, came into being. The Sinclair-Coulthard model encouraged a great deal of work along the same lines. Studies were made of samples of doctor-patient interviews, mother-child talk, committee meetings, etc.

Burton (1981: 61-81) has proposed modifications to the Sinclair-Coulthard model in order to make it suitable for analyzing conversation (see also Burton, 1980). Burton finds the concepts of EXCHANGE and MOVE most useful, but she changes the structure of EXCHANGE and reclassifies MOVES. She deletes the follow up MOVE, which occurs rarely in natural conversation, and gives two broad categories of MOVES: SUPPORTING and CHALLENGING. She also revises and reconsiders the list of ACTS, which come below MOVE on the rank scale in the Sinclair-Coulthard framework. I give below an example of Burton's (1981: 79) analysis with my rearrangement in the usual dialogue form:

	UTTERANCE	MOVE	ACT
A:	I'm going to do some weeding.	opening	informative
B:	Yes, please.	supporting	acknowledgement
A:	What?	challenging	
B:	Yes, please.	opening	
A:	You don't listen to anything I say.	opening	informative

Contd...

B: I thought you said challenging informative you were going to pour some drinks.

A: No, I said I'm going challenging informative to do some weeding.

I agree that the categories of MOVE and ACT are most useful in discourse analysis, but I would begin my analysis at the level of EXCHANGE. We first divide a dialogue into exchanges of different kinds. In a complete dialogue, we can recognize the following types: greetings, formulaic inquiries, customary exchange, interactive exchanges, closing, parting.[2]

The forms of greetings, formulaic inquiries, customary exchange, closing and parting are governed by cultural conventions. Interactive exchanges are the ones in which real interaction takes place. In these exchanges information is sought and given, advice is offered, comments are made, decisions are communicated, matters are thrashed out, personal differences are voiced and resolved. There may be more than one interactive exchange in a dialogue. Interactive exchanges can be separated on the basis of semantic domain if not grammar and pronunciation. The vocabulary of what may be called "common language" (Common English, for example) is analyzable in terms of domains and fields, and it should not be difficult to assign an exchange to a certain domain. Some syntactic and phonetic differences may also be present.

Dialogue Skills

Next we turn to what may be called dialogue skills; these are to be superposed to the usual language skills, and I leave the latter out of consideration. Salih (1983: 20-23) has listed five skills under the main heading "Dialogue Communicative Competence". These five skills are appropriateness of response, intelligibility, ease and dialogue fluency, role-playing, and turn-taking. I assented to this classification at the time that I supervised his research. I now feel that the first two skills are difficult to define and describe systematically, moreover, they are not specific to dialogue and are, indeed, taken care of elsewhere in language study.

I would like to begin with a new skill, namely mastery of the non-verbal signs used in dialogue, the culturally determined systems of gestures, facial expressions, eye contact, hand and finger movement, and non-linguistic vocal sounds—broadly defined, the kinesic system. Contrastive studies of such systems are rare, but there is a need to recognize the skill of using them. The second skill I would call "dialogue influency". We have seen how silence, hesitation, gestures, facial expressions, shrugging, nodding, shaking of the head all punctuate—or in another sense disrupt—the stream of linguistic sounds in a dialogue. A dialogue that has the linguistic fluency of a sermon or lecture would sound unnatural. Role-playing and turn-taking are important dialogue skills. They can be defined in linguistic and behavioural terms, although the task is again not an easy one. Roles define the nature and extent of participation. The power of directing the dialogue may rest with one of the participants according to his role, or be apportioned between the participants according to the relative importance of their roles in a given situation. Each culture lays down the conventions governing different roles, and a child picks up role-playing in the course of social interaction with guidance from the older members of the family and community. Turn-taking and turn-yielding are based on very complex behavioural and linguistic phenomena. The skills involve recognizing and learning the signals that indicate that the speaker has ended his turn. Similarly, non-linguistic behavioural signal, and some interruptions, or certain sounds, indicate that a participant is claiming his turn.

Three Illustrations

Below are three short dialogues to illustrate the points made in the foregoing discussion. I have recast the conversation in the usual dialogue form without naming the characters. The material has been taken from Penelope Mortimer's story "Saturday Lunch with the Brownings". I have suppressed the author's description and narration. It would be interesting to discover roles and study the structure of these dialogues. It may not be easy to recover the phonetic and kinesic dimensions of the dialogues, but an attempt can be made before consulting the source.

I

A: Hallo.

B: Hallo, Look what we got at the party.

A: Very nice, Was it a good party?

B: Quite, Rachel came too.

A: Jolly good, Where's Mummy?

B: Downstairs.

A: Well, good night then. Sleep well.

II

A: Hallo, How's it all going?

C: Oh, it's you.

A: I'm sorry about all that business this afternoon. Forget it.

C: Oh, that's all right. (Some activity) I suppose you don't know anything about the Gulf stream?

A: Nothing at all.

III

A: Hallo,

D: (*Silent*)

A: I've been asleep.

D: (*silent, engaged in work*)

A: Funny thing, I went out like a light. How do you feel?

D: (*silent, quiet activity*)

A: What's happening? What's the plan?

D: (*silent, turns head away*)

A: I've made it up with Rachel and C. I suppose it's going to take a good deal longer with you. Well, I suppose we can just sit here.

Teaching Dialogue

Our final concern is the teaching of dialogue. I have no intention of presenting a complete method. I wish to confine myself to certain aspects of dialogue teaching that arise out of our discussion. First of all, teacher must know that his final aim is not to teach the pupils how to act out a dialogue but to prepare them for participation in a natural dialogue situation. He must take up dialogue as an end and not merely as a means to teaching grammar, usage, and pronunciation. Secondly, the teacher should familiarize himself with discourse analysis. It is a well known principle in teaching that the material cannot be taught holistically. It must be broken down into small units and skills for presentation to the class. The units and skills must be identified according to some theoretical framework. In the third place, dialogue involves not only teaching linguistic forms but also the communicative behaviour patterns that form an important dimension of natural conversation: shrugging the shoulders and various kinds of eye contact are as important as intonation and vocabulary, and their use and function must be presented to the pupils with proper contextualization. In the beginning of the course, the dialogue components can be taken up one by one. The teacher must systematically prepare the subject in this way before he approaches the class with a lesson.

The importance of audio-visual aids in dialogue teaching cannot be overemphasized; dialogue can never be taught properly without these aids. Television lessons and recorded dialogues on videotapes are very helpful. The role of the teacher himself and real participants, however, should not be overlooked. They themselves provide an excellent audio-visual aid. For this, however, the teacher should be well trained by specialists or native speakers. Unfortunately, this is not happening, so we have to fall back on mechanical and electronic aids. A good idea would be to prepare a course on dialogue for television broadcast to schools and colleges, with the time schedule announced well in advance.

At the presentation stage, the problem is how to begin most effectively. I suggest the teacher should begin with a metadialogue, or an introductory dialogue, greeting the pupils and then asking carefully chosen questions about dialogue; or introducing the subject-matter of the dialogue he is going to teach and asking some pertinent questions that draw attention to dialogue components and dialogue skills. The teacher must present a whole dialogue in the first lesson, but the dialogue, apart from the usual components, should contain only one interactive exchange. Thereafter, he can take up the components and skills for separate treatment and practice. Grant Taylor (1975) has done something along these lines in his English Conversation Practice. He has grouped the exercise dialogues under such headings as "Meeting" and "Parting" and has arranged typical interactive exchanges according to topics or domains.

Finally, the pupils must be encouraged to participate in—or rather cope with—real dialogue situations. They must be thrown, as it were, into conversation and allowed to fend for themselves. You can never predict what questions are going to be asked or what topics are going to come up. The student must prepare himself for this unique feature of natural dialogue, and he must be helped to achieve this goal, without which dialogue as discourse cannot be said to have been learned.

The Need for Further Study

The study of dialogue as a form of discourse is in its infancy. The subject is complex and requires further study and research. And teaching dialogue involves a hundred other things. It is not easy to master dialogue as a socio-linguistic phenomenon in a foreign language, and this article does no more than indicate the difficulties involved and point to a possible but partial solution. The full task requires a collaborative effort on the part of linguists, sociologists, psychologists, methodologists, and language teachers and pupils.

Notes

1. See Sahab Abdul Aziz Salih (1983). The plan of the work which included a pedagogic experiment along with chapter division was made under my supervision. When I left for India in June 1982, the guidance was taken over by a local teacher, subsequently chapters were sent to me for correction.

2. See Salih (1983: 25-28) for a similar analysis into what he calls components.

Works Cited

Allen, Harold B., and Russell N. Campbell (1978). *Teaching English as a Second Language.* New Delhi: Tata McGraw-Hill.

Allen, J.P.B., and S. Pit Corder, eds. (1975). *Papers in Applied Linguistics.* Oxford: Oxford University Press.

Benett, W.A. 1968. *Aspects of Language and Language Teaching.* London: Cambridge University Press.

Bright, J.A., and G.P. McGregor (1978). *Teaching English as a Second Language.* London: English Language Book Society.

Burton, Deirdre (1980). *Dialogue and Discourse.* London: Routledge and Kegan Paul.

—— (1981). "Analyzing Spoken Discourse". In *Studies in Discourse Analysis.* See Coulthard and Montgomery 1981.

Coulthard, Malcolm, and Martin Montgomery, ed. (1981). *Studies in Discourse Analysis.* London: Routledge and Kegan Paul.

Criper, C. and H.G. Widdowson (1975). "Socio-linguistics and Language Teaching". In *Papers in Applied Linguistics.* See Allen and Corder, 1975.

Gosling, John (1981). "Kinesics in Discourse". In *Studies in Discourse Analysis.* See Coulthard and Montgomery 1981.

Lado, Robert (1977). *Language Teaching: A Scientific Approach.* New Delhi: Tata McGraw-Hill.

Mortimer, Penelpoe (1977). *Saturday Lunch with the Brownings and Other Stories.* Harmondsworth: Penguin.

Newmark, Gerald and Edward Diler (1978). "Emphasizing the Audio in the Audio-Lingual Approach". In *Teaching English as a Second Language.* See Allen and Campbell 1978.

Salih, Sahab Abdul Aziz (1983). The Teaching of Dialogue with Reference to the New Course for Iraq. Unpublished MA Thesis, University of Basrah.

Sinclair, J. and R.M. Coulthard (1975). *Towards an Analysis of Discourse.* London: Oxford University Press.

Taylor, Grant (1975). *English Conversation Practice.* New Delhi: Tata McGraw-Hill.

Teaching Poetry: A Linguistic Method

14

A linguistic method of teaching poetry presupposes a linguistic theory of poetry as well as an analytical framework; neither of these are available in a standard form—so much the better, some would think, where poetry is concerned. Rather than struggle with the difficult—and, perhaps, not so desirable—task of attempting a scientific definition of poetry, authors on literary linguistics have mostly concentrated their efforts on characterizing the language of poetry, assuming that all that matters in a poem is its language (Hill, 1958; Jakobson, in Sebeok, 1960; Levin, 1961; Nowottny, 1962; Leech, 1969). A number of analyses of individual poems have also appeared (Hill, 1955; Leech, 1965; Sinclair, in Fowler, 1966; Halliday, 1966). I have also dealt with theoretical issues and attempted to develop an analytical model (Sharma, 1982b, 1985a, 1985b). The pedagogical aspects of the framework, I have proposed, are discussed in my paper, "Analysing a Poem: A Linguistic-Pedagogical Approach" (1982a).

My aim in the present paper, however, is not to reopen any theoretical or analytical issues, but to concentrate on the method of presentation, except where theoretical elucidation is absolutely necessary for justifying the method. One requirement for the teacher, though, is a knowledge of the theoretical background such as it is, and a prior linguistic

---

New Directions in English Language Teaching, Ed. Ashok K. Jha and Rajul Bhargava. Jaipur: Pointer Publishers, 1988.

analysis of the poem he is going to teach. Before I describe the steps in presentation, I wish to submit that the method is worth serious consideration for three reasons. First, it is logically based on the foundations of a linguistic view of poetry and its linguistic analysis. Second, it has been partially tried by me with some measure of effectiveness although, I must hasten to add, its complete success, at this stage, cannot be asserted. Third, the method is bound to create an awareness of finer linguistic distinctions in the learner, although it does not proceed with the spurious intent of teaching both language and poetry or language through poetry—the finer points of grammar and meaning which get taught do not form part of ordinary English language teaching. On this issue I share the view of Halliday *et al.* that no student should be "pushed into literary work until he has sufficient linguistic ability to understand, enjoy and appreciate the literary texts that he will be studying" (1964: 184-85). Rhymes and simple didactic, narrative or descriptive verse introduced at an early stage are another matter and cannot properly be regarded as the teaching of poetry.

We are now ready to deal with the problem of presentation step by step. For the teaching material, I have chosen a short poem called "A Coat" by W.B. Yeats.

Step I: Context of Situation

A common complaint against the traditional 'scholarly' method of teaching poetry is that the teacher devotes most of his time to discussing the biographical, social and literary background and very little time is given to the poem itself. The charge is justified, for a poem, as a stimulus, seeks to recreate a unique experience: a poem does not simply mean, it happens to the reader as it happened to the poet. The poem itself ought to be the focus of the lesson and the objective, an experience and not the background. The other extreme is exemplified by the view held by Bright and McGregor whose model lesson begins directly with a reading of the poem, without any introduction, because what is not in the poem does not matter (1978: 222). This line of thinking is equally unbalanced and militates against the linguistic theory, for a message acquires its meaning and produces the intended effect by reference to its context of situation. "Context of situation", says Firth, "is best used as a suitable schematic construct to apply to language events, and that it is a group of related categories at a different level from grammatical categories but rather of the same abstract nature" (1957: 182). Halliday *et al.* treat context as one of the three principal levels of language analysis: "The context is the relation of language, which is in fact a relation of its internal patterns, its 'form', to other features of the situations in which language operates" (1964: 10). It has not been easy to define context of situation scientifically as a schematic construct, but for practical teaching purposes, we can always identify the elements which are vital to the understanding of a poem: only these elements have to be introduced in the beginning. This procedure can function as an effective control on the endless forays of the traditional teacher into history, biography, and what not.

For the poem under discussion, I would give the following context of situation. W.B. Yeats belongs to the older generation of modern poets. He was born in 1865. His poetic career falls into two major phases. He began writing in a romantic manner, recreating, beautiful landscapes and mythological incidents. Round about 1914, when this poem was written, he was worried by the imitations of his poetry. Also, the troubled political scene in Ireland and Europe prompted him to change his themes and style: he felt the need for dealing with hard realities in a language which is not mere decoration and is closer to the living speech of men.

It should be noted here that a piece of creative writing has two contexts: one external, I mean external to the work, and the other, internal. We have just presented the external or communicative context in which the poet addresses the reader, the poem itself being the message. The internal context is the situation imaginatively created by the poet, for example, Ulysses in his old age sitting and meditating on his ambition to sail beyond the seas. The internal context itself is part of the message and emerges in the course of reading.

Step II: Reading of the Poem (Optional)

This reading is done by the teacher. Most specialists would agree on this step and would even insist that this should be the first step. I have often achieved good results by postponing it until I have dealt with the poem bit by bit. This unusual procedure, I guess, calls for some justification.

A work of literature differs from a painting or statue in that it has a dynamic existence in time—"a reader, like a hearer, must decode in a fixed order—the text, for both, is not a static object, but a dynamic phenomenon, something which is EXPERIENCED IN TIME" (Leech and Short 1981: 211). In normal reading the poem unfolds itself gradually and at every turn there are surprises and complexities to be encountered. A native reader is competent enough to take in this onrush of experience in quick succession as the reading proceeds. But a foreign learner can seldom do so. He has to be brought near to the native reader's ability in order that he may really enjoy the poem. This can be done by teaching the poem piece by piece—line by line and sentence by sentence. I have also found that the surprises and challenges which account for the effect of the poem and occur in a sequence, help maintain the students' interest and curiosity. This process gives something of the thrill of a hurdle race. I therefore prefer the reading of the poem after the explication is completed.

Step III: Discussion of the Title

The title, as I have suggested elsewhere, represents the semantic chunk out of which the poet carves out an aesthetic experience (1982a: 52; 1985a: 17-25). Its denotative and connotative content deserves a most careful study. The teacher may elicit the full meaning of the phrase 'a coat' by asking the students to contrast it with 'the coat' and 'coats'. It is not for nothing that Wordsworth used the plural 'Daffodils' for his well-known poem and Ted Hughes used the title 'Snowdrop' for a poem in which he describes his subject as an individual engaged in a grim battle against winter. It would be interesting to compare this latter poem with one by Walter De La Mare with the title 'The Snowdrop'. These titles have different meanings based on grammatical distinctions and raise different perceptual images in the mind of the reader. The teacher himself need not employ the technical vocabulary of linguistic analysis; he can always bring out the distinctions by contextualisation. A further point in this case is the referential meaning of 'coat', which is misapplied by many Indians to what is a 'jacket' in British usage. Some visual aids or realia could be used to clarify the meaning as it is crucial for this poem. Otherwise, the student is bound to be puzzled later by the expression 'from heel to throat'.

Step IV: Progress Through the Poem

This stage consists of exploration of the poetic experience by means of question-answer and exploitation of audio-visual and reference material. But first the units. Poetry is organised at two levels—linguistic and discoursal. At the linguistic level, the sentence is the maximal unit; at the level of poetic discourse, the stanza or verse paragraph is the maximal unit. The stanza is divided into lines or verses. At the discourse level, we have also to consider schemes, tropes and symbolism. Poetry is also characterised by deviation, deviance and patterning. We have to study all these, but not as units. For units, we shall do well to choose the line and the sentence because, at their respective levels, each has clear boundary markers and the sentence has the advantage of giving the complete sense. So the teacher reads the first line:

I MADE my song a coat

John Unterecker has rightly pointed out that this expression is ambiguous, "which the reader, if acute, is bound to struggle with" (1959: 34). However, his suggestion that both the senses are acceptable cannot be defended. But the teacher has to explain both the possibilities, although in the long run only one of them will be applicable. He can do so by asking the students to recast the sentence according to each meaning separately:

I made a coat for my song

I made a coat out of my song

or give a clear example of each underlying structure:

We gave him a prize

We elected him a member

The second problem is the metaphor of coat, which is the cornerstone of the whole poem: here I think the method I have proposed for detection and analysis of metaphor will be of great practical help (1982b). Leaving the technicalities aside, the simple procedure may be stated thus: proceed in your reading as far as the literal meaning carries you and stop at the item which appears to subvert the literal interpretation; then read backwards and consider the transfer of semantic features which would resolve the tangle. In the present case, we stop at 'coat', read backwards and examine the various meanings and semantic features of 'song' and 'coat'. In the course of this exercise it will be revealed that 'song' means 'the poetic experience', which is dressed, as it were, in language, that 'coat' is a garment for the body and so language is to a song (poetry) what a coat is to a person. The verb 'MADE' (='made for') and the noun 'coat' lead to what is called personification: a thing is made for somebody, a coat worn by somebody. This process of humanizing is linguistically more complex and it has been described at some length in my paper, "Anthropomorphism in the Language of Poetry".

We have also to pay attention to cohesion. Gutwinski has discussed cohesion in literary texts (1976). I have shown how subtle and deep-set, or circuitous, it can be (1985a: 41-46). However, the cohesion between the title and the first line of this poem is simple: by means of repetition of 'a coat'. Later the metaphor itself by semantic association serves to achieve cohesion. We move on to the line:

Covered with embroideries

From now onwards the two levels of meaning run together. This phrase literally describes the coat, but we have to transfer its meaning to poetry. The word 'embroideries' suggests decoration in designs or figures and itself stands out as an ornament among common words of one or two syllables. The two lines should be read together and the variation in rhythm made clear. The plural form gives a concrete meaning in the sense of an ornamental figure.

Out of old mythologies

This phrase qualifies 'embroideries' and we run into a double metaphor. 'Mythology' has a dreamy romantic connotation and also is foregrounded in its setting; the plural, again, points to stories with characters and plots: we are transported into the twilight of history. The distinction between 'myth' and 'mythology' has to be explained by questioning and contextualization. The word 'old' is also significant.

From heel to throat;

The student must be made to realize the nature of this modification. The coat is covered with embroideries from heel to throat. The abstract modifier 'completely' is described in concrete terms. Does it apply to 'song'? Perhaps, and in that case the other interpretation of the first line (song = coat) would hold good. The rhythm is that of the first line, but with only two feet.

But the fools caught it,

Both the words and rhythm signal a change. Mark the juxtaposition of two stressed syllables, which produces a jarring note, suggesting the awkwardness of the imitations. All the words are common words. The students may be asked to guess the true referent of 'the fools'.

Wore it in the world's eyes

The flat connotation of 'Wore' has to be realised as well as the suggestive meaning of "in the world's eyes": the idea of impudence on the part of the imitators.

As though they'd wrought it.

The use of the connective 'As though' has to be explained. 'Wrought' is a hackneyed literary use.

Song, let them take it,

The apostrophe and a change of sentence type from declarative to imperative make another, and more important, turn; the style is in clear contrast with that of the first and second sections; it does not have the artificialities of either kind.

For there's more enterprise.

'Enterprise' stands out by its length and by its use as an uncountable noun. The difference in meaning between the singular and the plural ought to be discussed. The word combines the ideas of courage, achievement of art and adventure. These finer points ought to be brought home.

In walking naked

'Naked' is the keyword. It does not necessarily mean 'without any kind of clothing, whatsoever'. Still the word is quite startling. It conveys a deeper meaning here, which can be inferred. It implies lack of artificiality or ornamentation; it suggests that the body has its own beauty, a kind of organic form which no decoration can surpass; it also suggests economy of expression embodied in the three words of the line itself. 'Walk' is an active verb (in clear contrast with 'sit' or 'lie') suggesting the dynamic nature of the poetic process. There are many other aspects and points of explication which I have omitted. The depth to which you explore the poem will depend on the level and motivation of the class.

Step V: Reading of the Poem

Our students are now ready to enjoy the poem when it is read to them as a whole. The teacher has to read the poem with proper expressive pronunciation and enunciation, rehearsed beforehand.

Step VI: Linguistic Form

I have presented the idea of the linguistic 'pictures' of a poem showing that these abstracts of its form help us imbibe the total effect of the poem along certain dimensions e.g. concrete-abstract, general-specific, dynamic-static, sensuous-conceptual; they also lead us to a recognition of the linguistic patterning of the poem (1982a, 1985a). Constructing these pictures offers a great deal of language work to the advanced student. At any rate if the teacher has already worked out these pictures, he can always discuss them in a non-technical language.

The following are two syntactic pictures of the poem at different levels:

(i) S_{decl}

S_{imp}

(ii) S V O_i O_d

Adj P

Adv P

Conn S V O

V O Adv P

Adv Cl

Voc Vo Adv P

Picture (i) shows a declarative followed by an imperative. The declarative has an informative function: it states something; the imperative is associated with resolutions and power. Thus the turn of thought we have noticed earlier is clearly confirmed by this syntactic shift. Picture (ii) takes us deeper into the design of the poem. The first sentence falls into two parts. The first of these, with its three modifying phrases, suggests preciosity and mirrors the first motif. The second part is a variation of the first; it projects the idea of mere imitation. In fact the details of modification in the first clause reveal greater complexity. 'Coat' is qualified by the whole of the remaining part ('covered...throat'); 'embroideries' is qualified by the following phrase ('out of ...mythologies') which is structurally ambiguous and the last phrase modifies 'covered'. In contrast, the second sentence in the imperative has a simpler structure showing in actual practice the poet's new attitudes to his calling. We have seen that there is a parallel choice of vocabulary items in consonance with the theme of each section.

Let us take for comparison a short poem by Stephen Spender on a similar theme:

The word bites like a fish.
Shall I throw it back free
Arrowing to that sea

Where thoughts lash tail and fin?
Or shall I pull it in
To rhyme upon a dish?

The sentence picture is: S_{decl} S_{inter} S_{inter}. The two alternative yes/no questions, which remain unanswered, throw up the poet's dilemma about the poem in his mind: should he give it a linguistic shape and serve to the readers like fish or should he let it jump back into the subconscious which is its home? (The unconscious and subconscious parts of the mind are often symbolised by the sea.)

We can also construct semantic pictures representing the distribution of structure and content words, general and specific words and denotative and connotative words. They will define the figure the poem makes on the reader's mind: the 'feel' of the poem in sensuous terms. I shall not go into these details, but I have said enough to serve as guideline for completing the study of a poem as experience.

Step VII: Appreciation

This will take the form of a group discussion on the poem as a whole—its theme, structure, sound patterns, etc.—followed by evaluation.

Reference Tools

In the foregoing pages, we have in a way also dealt with the skill of reading a poem. Our ultimate aim should be to impart to the student the ability to read and enjoy a poem by himself. When a student tries to read an English poem by himself, he will be in need of some reference books and a dictionary. The teacher has to acquaint him with this material and its use. I have found the following kinds of reference material necessary:

1. **Dictionary**: The OED is the best. It supplies not only modern but also older meanings of a word. In addition, a good dictionary of current English will also be needed for reading contemporary poetry.

2. **Encyclopaedia:** A one-volume encyclopaedia such as *Collins* Concise Encyclopaedia would be sufficient in most cases. The student can find out the names of persons and places used in the poem. For some poems, e.g. those by Eliot, he may have to go to a bigger encyclopaedia.
3. **A history of the English language:** The English language has changed considerably since the Old English period in structure and vocabulary. In Shakespeare's English, for example, the words, 'aspect' and 'character' had a different stress pattern and he used the pronoun 'his' for inanimate objects. A.C. Bough's *A History of the English Language* is quite comprehensive and easily available.
4. **A glossary of literary terms:** A glossary or dictionary of literature gives useful information about forms of literature, trends, prosody and rhetorical devices used in poetry. The following two are widely consulted:
    1. *Dictionary of World Literature,* ed. J.T. Shipley.
    2. *A Glossary of Literary Terms,* M.H. Abrams.

A third book (*A Dictionary of Modern Critical Terms*) edited by Roger Fowler takes into account the linguistic approach and includes such terms as 'foregrounding', 'deviation' and 'syntax'.

Works Cited

Bright, J.A. and McGregor, G.P. (1978). *Teaching English as a Second Language.* London: ELBS.

Firth, J.R. (1957). *Papers in Linguistics* 1934-41. London: Oxford University Press.

Fowler, R. (1966). (ed). *Essays on Style and Language.* London: Routledge and Kegan Paul.

Gutwinski, W. (1976). *Cohesion in Literary Texts.* The Hague: Mouton.

Halliday, M.A.K. (1966). 'Descriptive Linguistics in Literary Studies', in *Patterns in language: Papers in General, Descriptive and Applied Linguistics*, M.A.K. Halliday and Angus McIntosh, London: Longman.

Halliday, M.A.K., McIntosh, A. and Strevens, P. (1964). *The Linguistic Sciences and Language Teaching.* London: ELBS.

Hill, A.A. (1955). "Analysis of *The Windhover*. An Experiment in Structural Method". *Publications of the Modern Language Association* 70.

—— (1958). "A Program for the Definition of Literature", *Texas Studies in English* 37.

Jakobson, R.C. (1960). "Closing Statement: Linguistics and Poetics". In *Style in Language,* ed. Sebeok. Cambridge, Mass: MIT Press.

Leech, G.N. (1965). "This Bread I Break'—Language and Interpretation". *A Review of English Literature,* 6, 2.

—— (1969). *A Linguistics Guide to English Poetry*. London: Longman.

Leech, G.N. and Michael Short (1981). *Style in Fiction. A Linguistic Introduction to English Fictional Prose*. London: Longman.

Levin, S.R. (1962). *Linguistic Structures in Poetry*. The Hague: Mouton.

Nowottny, Winifred (1962). *The Language Poets Use*. London: The Athlone Press.

Sebeok, T.A. (1960) (ed). *Style in Language*. Cambridge, Mass: MIT Press.

Sharma R.S. (1982a). "Analysing a Poem: A Linguistic-Pedagogical Approach", in *The Twofold Voice: Essays in Honour of Ramesh Mohan*, ed. S.NA. Rizvi. Universitat Salzburg.

—— (1982). Metaphor "Analysis and Interpretation". *Indian Linguistics,* Vol. 43. Nos. 3-4.

—— (1985a). *Linguistic Aspects of Contemporary English Poetry*. Varanasi: Academic Publishers.

—— (1985b). "Teaching Semantic Distinctions through Literature," *IRAL* XXIII/3.

Sinclair, I. McH. (1966). "Taking a Poem to Pieces". In Roger Fowler.

Unterecker, John (1959). *A Reader's Guide to W.B. Yeats,* London: Thames and Hudson.

Analyzing a Poem: A Linguistic-Pedagogical Approach

15

I

Analysis and interpretation of a poem can no longer be treated in vacuo on an ad hoc basis or as a matter of personal insight and understanding alone. The task is best attempted within a theoretical framework. By theoretical framework I mean a conceptual base as regards the nature, function and structure of poetry in general and a poem in particular. "Perception", observes Walter A. Davis, "is never unmediated". According to him even the minute observations we make are theory bound and "the problem is not to cleanse oneself of concepts but to discover one's concepts—and then to enquire as deeply as one can into their grounds".[1] Further there is no incompatibility between theory and practice: our analysis and interpretation are governed by theory: they receive direction from it as well as a scientific status with the possibility of objective verification as far as possible in empirical studies.

My aim in this paper is to propose a practically-oriented model for analysis and interpretation of a poem, which offers certain pedagogical advantages. It involves linguistic analysis of a certain kind and is intended for advanced classes. Now,

---

An abridged version published in *The Twofold Voice Essays in Honour of Ramesh Mohan*. Ed. S.N.A. Rizzvi, Universitat Salzburg, 1982.

literary scholarship is generally opposed to this kind of study: it is assumed that in taking a poem to pieces we destroy its beauty or aesthetic effect. This, I believe, is unfair; analysis for its own sake may not yield much, but it is not inimical to literary experience by its very nature: on the contrary, if used as a means, analysis can lead to a deeper and surer understanding of poems. Stylisticians have argued that certain intuitive labels such as the "grand style" of Milton, often employed by the literary critic, can be given specific formulation on the basis of linguistic analysis. Where analysis is made as a preliminary to interpretation and presentation before an audience, there need be no objection to it at all. Introducing her book on the study of poetry (not linguistic, strictly speaking), Marjorie Boulton has pointed out that "the only sound reason for examining poetry technically is that this adds to our enjoyment".[2]

Let us now turn to the second aspect, namely, teaching. What do we mean by teaching poetry? Does it mean imparting knowledge about poetry as such or discussing all the poems written in English? I would say, neither. The first task is vaguely philosophical and the second well nigh impossible. Our aim in teaching poetry is to train the student in the art or science of recovering the message encoded by the poet. "In other words, our primary duty is not so much the teaching of knowledge about literature as the imparting of skill in the recognition and comprehension of literary modes of meaning."[3] The message itself is a highly complex experience; it is not a simple unit of information or affective state. The traditional method of teaching which consists largely of background discussion and historical scholarship—that is, talking round and round the poem—fails to arouse the student to a proper response. Commenting on historical sense, I.A. Richards has observed: "Its prime aim is just to help us to read better. But somehow all this wealth of scholarly aid does not lift up our hearts as it should."[4]

This lifting up of our hearts—a literary way of referring to the experience of a poem or a piece of literature—particularly requires motivation. Motivation represents an assortment of forces which impel and encourage the learner to pursue the goal. Motivation "not only instigates behaviour but also operates to reinforce ongoing behaviour".[5] Curiosity, challenge, the desire for competence and longing for discovery are among intrinsic motives which do not depend on outside reinforcement to the activity they support. Reward lies in the successful achievement of the goal or even in the activity itself. Reading of poetry is an ideal activity for this kind of motivation and if the teacher fails to elicit more than a few yawns and general drowsiness, there must be something seriously wrong with the guiding tenets and preparatory material of poetry teaching. There are grounds to believe that a linguistically oriented analytical approach can ensure the kind of motivation I have been discussing. These grounds will become clearer as we proceed. Another advantage of such an approach is the possibility of transfer of learning. The student can make a gratifying use of his knowledge of grammar and linguistics (where it is taught as a subject) in the poetry class. It will also encourage student participation since the learner is expected to analyse the form and discover the poetic meaning and effect of linguistic structures.

The first problem to be tackled in any approach to poetry is its nature and function. From Aristotle down to I.A. Richards, scholars have proposed all kinds of theories and yet the subject is as controversial as ever. For any workable model, it is absolutely necessary to take a modest and sensible view of the matter. Without losing ourselves into philosophical depths, we can agree that poetry affords us a certain kind of satisfaction and that proper enjoyment of poetry is a mark of being civilised. Reading or hearing of a poem creates in us a certain kind of mood with a remarkable mixture of thought and emotion. This mood may be of sadness or gaiety, elation, frustration or excitements, a profound awareness of loss or beauty. The important thing to be realised, as we shall see later, is that whatever the mood, it is definable in terms of the language used rather than some *a priori* principles. "Poetry", says Michael Roberts, "may be intended to amuse, or to ridicule, or to persuade, or to produce an effect which we feel to be more valuable than amusement and different from instruction; but primarily poetry is an exploration of the possibilities of language".[6] If our aim is to consider the language of poetry "it is prudent to begin with what is 'there' in the poem—'there' in the sense that it can be described and referred to as unarguably given by the words".[7] The pendulum has swung to the other extreme. Some enthusiastic E.L.T. experts have pleaded for cutting out the introductory remarks altogether, not to talk of the poet's biography, literary background, historical setting, etc. After presenting a sample lesson, Bright and McGregor add the following remarks:

> In the lesson we have just watched we note the absence of introduction. It began with the reading of a poem not with a statement of who wrote it and certainly not with a mine of information about why, where and when he wrote it and how it relates to the rest of his work. If all this is not in the poem then it does not matter at this stage of literary education, nor, we suspect, at many other stages.[8]

I cannot help thinking that this is a naive view based on an imperfect understanding of linguistic theory. A piece of language always has meaning in the light of its "context of situation" and in normal intercourse where language is used, we do have a prior knowledge of participants and properties. If a poem, as a piece of language, has a message, then we must gather some idea of the relevant factors of the situation. This, by no means, will give a free rein to the teacher's irrelevant and distorting disquisitions which hinder the proper enjoyment of a poem. The concept of context of situation offers a necessary scientific basis for the selection of introductory material. There are cogent reasons, in my view, to hold that the rendering and discussion of a poem should be preceded by a careful presentation of the context. In this connection, I find the remarks of Robert Lado most sensible. Discussing the teaching of Carl Sandburg's poem "Chicago" he says:

> The students should find out before they read the poem that Carl Sandburg was born in Illinois, so that Chicago is not only his city as an American but as a son of its state. He worked as a laborer, porter

> dishwasher, newspaperman, and editor there. He loves it as it is.

The student should know something about Chicago as a transportation centre. He further adds:

> How much to explain will depend on the students and the time available. Too much explanation will kill the students' interest in the poem.[9]

I would, however, hesitate to subscribe to the last remarks above and say that what determines the amount of background information to be given is the requirement of the context without which the poem will fail to render its full meaning. Sometimes there are things in a poem which no amount of linguistic analysis can clarify, e.g. Comus' ancestry in Milton's masque of that name.[10]

Some linguists hold that a work of literature provides its own framework of events and "whatever the role attempted or achieved by literature in society as language it is self-sufficient and self-contextualizing".[11] This, again, is a simplistic view, undermining the status of literature as communication. It would be, perhaps, nearer the truth to say that literature has a double context—internal and external. Where the poet speaks in his own person (this is by no means always easy to decide) without a 'persona' or narrator role, the two contexts will coincide. For example, in "La Belle Dame Sans Merci" by John Keats the two contexts ought to be considered separately; in his Sonnet, "Bright Star: Would I were steadfast as thou art" they overlap. It is important to note here that whereas the external context provides the framework to the message, the internal context forms part of it and must be interpreted accordingly.

Next, we must consider the dynamic nature of poetic experience. A poem takes place in time as an event before it enters the timeless world of aesthetic values. In this respect it differs from a painting or a statue, the whole of which you can see at a glance. Apart from the fact that the material of poetry is language itself, it has a continuously growing pattern. In a diagrammatic representation of the events which take place in reading a poem, we have to depict the eye as reading a succession of printed words giving rise to a stream of reaction.[12] Discussing the nature of the poet's creative effort C. Day Lewis says:

> If he has to work in this hand-to-mouth way, it is because a poem is an organic growth in which the theme only reveals itself through the growing pattern.[13]

Here is a warning for the linguists interested in the analysis of literature. If you compute the ratios and proportions of linguistic features in a poem, you may offer clues to the total effect, for example, nominality or verbality, which may be correlated with static and dynamic nature of the experience respectively; but you are ignoring a more vital complementary task, namely, the dynamic distribution of linguistic features, and it is the latter which accounts for the experience of a poem as it is read. Let me make this clear by examining a concrete example.

In making a linguistic analysis of "Leda and the Swan" by W.B. Yeats, Halliday discovers a preponderance of nominal groups in the poem.[14] This is an important finding which certainly accounts for a certain kind of impact. But we cannot stop at that. We must examine how the nominal groups occur relative to the verb from line to line and watch constantly the level of low verbality rise and fall and rise again. The poem opens with a nominal group (a highly condensed verbless clause), then a weak verbal element is introduced by using participial forms which maintains its level until a finite verb is met with in the last verse of stanza 1. The point, I have tried to make, is, I think, sufficiently clear and I need not discuss the whole poem.

Rather, I would now like to approach the crux of the problem: the dynamic structure of a poem. Making due allowance for the context of situation, our real experience of the poem begins with the title (If there isn't any, which is rare, with the first sentence). The semantic and grammatical composition of the title must be carefully studied. The student must explore all the meanings of the title and all types of meaning: referential, affective, stylistic, etc. Except for internal poetic treatment as in "Love's Alchemy" or "The Loveliness of Love", the title must be discussed from the common point of view, the meanings as given in the dictionary. There is, however, one additional general point. As soon as we know that a word or phrase is the title of the poem, i.e. it belongs to the poetic register, we must be prepared for the possibility of new turns in its meaning and significance. Figuratively speaking, the title represents the semantic chunk, like the potter's clay or the sculptor's block, out of which the poet is going to form an aesthetic utterance by using addition, subtraction, generalisation, specialization, enrichment, condensation, expansion or inflation, etc.

The title, therefore, is of prime importance. Marjorie Boulton has demonstrated this by a small experiment. She quotes George Herbert's poem "Redemption" without the title. The result is that several expressions in the poem become puzzling, absurd or nonsensical. Once the title is revealed, the poem regains its coherence and beauty.[15] I.A. Richards also insists on paying full attention to the title saying that the title has "a great deal to do with the poem".[16]

The first sentence of the poem follows the title: it is the second part of the poem. It presents some kind of proposition, though not in a strict logical sense. The first sentence has to be taken as a unit by virtue of its unique position. It initiates the poetic discourse and is an important pointer to the direction the poem may take. Unlike the title, it is closely linked with the rest of the poem and is like the headword in a group to be modified by what follows. It may or may not be tied to the title by linguistic cohesion.

What remains is the third part irrespective of stanza divisions, although the latter are not without significance as regards the structure of the poem. At this point, I must hark back to the dynamic nature of the poem. The third part progressively modifies the first proposition and ought to be watched at every turn. The final picture crystallizes as a result of the linguistic manipulations employed by the poet, but, as suggested earlier, the continuously changing stimulation by linguistic means is responsible for our experience of the poem.

Two things ought to be noted. My discussion of the dynamic structure of the poem has so far remained theoretical.

This is so because I have reserved its application for the last section of the paper in which I attempt an interpretation of Ted Hughes' poem "Snowdrop" on the basis of a linguistic analysis which is to follow. Secondly, the model applies to short poem of the type generally included in anthologies and course books.

II

Some explanatory remarks ought to be prefaced to the analysis. I have attempted a line by line detailed analysis followed by what I call linguistic pictures of the poem. I admit that all the details given may not be relevant, but in a model aiming at a degree of comprehensiveness, they cannot be excluded. For grammatical analysis, I have made use of *A Grammar of Contemporary English* by R. Quirk, S. Greenbaum, G. Leech and J. Svartvik up to a certain extent. The book has a great merit for stylistic analysis since it has covered some semantic aspects of English Grammar. As will be clear, I have also depended on other works as well as my own insight. Ideally, I assume that both general/specific and abstract/concrete distinctions can be extended to nearly all word-classes, although I have not done so in my analysis. I have split 'concrete' into two and have also given weight to psychological intensity in marking words as 'concrete', in addition to physical reality.

The abbreviations used in the analysis, I hope, will not present any difficulty to those familiar with traditional and modern English Grammar and with common semantic categories. For guidance, abbreviations are explained in the analysis of the title.

Snowdrop

Now is the globe shrunk tight
Round the mouse's dulled wintering heart.
Weasel and crow, as if moulded in brass,
Move through an outer darkness
Not in their right minds,
With the other deaths. She, too, pursues her ends,
Brutal as the stars of this month,

Her pale head heavy as metal.

—Ted Hughes

Analysis

–
–
–
–
–

N (noun)
Co (common noun)
sing (singular)
mf+mf (free morpheme)
Snowdrop
C (Content word)
Con (Connotation)
f (favourable)
gen (generic)
Conc 1 (Concrete)
nature (flowers) (register)
Non-Normal
Declarative
Simple

A		S		V	A
Adv		Noun Phrase mh		Verb Phrase	Adj
Adv Adjunct time point	v aux pass	art def hom	N Com Co sing	v passive dyn. process intr	Adj start gradable inherent (adjunct) (manner)
mf	mf	mf	mf	mf	mf
Now	is	the	globe	shrunk	tight

c	s	s		c		c		c
Den	–	–		Den n		conunf		Can unf
Sp	–	–		Sp(U)		Sp		(Contd...)
Conc 2	–	–		Conc 1 nature		Conc 2		Conc 2
Prep		Noun (m) mmmh		Phrase				
Prep stat	art def hom	N Com Co	–	v dyn. process intr P.P.		v dyn. process intr Progr		N Com CO
mf	mf	mf	mb infl pl.	mf	mb infl P.P.	mf	mb progr	mf
Round	the	mouse's		dulled		wintering		heart
s	s	c		c		c		c
–	—	Den n		Con unf		Con unf		Con f
		Sp(Gen)		Sp		Sp		Sp
		Conc 1		Conc 2		Conc 2		Conc 1
		Animal Kingdom		environmental impact		environmental impact		body parts

Non-normal

Declarative

Complex

S		A					
		Elliptical clause				Manner	
Non phrase h+h		Subordinator			Participial		Phrase
N Con Co	Conj	N Com Co	Subordinator hypothetical comparison		v dyn process- tr P.P.	prep stat	N Com m
mf	mf	mf	mf	mf	mb infl P.P.	mf	mf
Weasel	and	Crow	as	if	moulded	in	brass,
c	s	c	s	s	c	s	c
Den n	–	Den n	–	–	Den n	–	Den n
Gen	–	Gen	–	–	Sp	–	Sp
Conc 1	–	Conc 1	–	–	Conc 2	–	Conc 1
Animal kingdom		bird family	–	–	manufacturing		metals
V					A		

					of place		
V	Prep					Noun phrase	
						m m h	
v dyn	prep	art indef			Adj stat		N Com
transitional	dyn				non-g non		m
event	passage				inherent		
intr							
mf	mf		mf	mf	mf der	mf	mb der
Move	through		an		outer	darkness	
c	s		s		c	c	
Den n	–		–		Den n	Conunf	
Gen n	–		–		Sp	Gen	
Conc 2	–		–		Conc 2	Conc 2	
motion	–		–		relative	natural	
					spatial	phenomena	
					position		

A

(Adv. Clause, Manner, Elliptical)

Adv	Prep		Noun Phrase		
			m m h		
Adv	prep stat	Adj	Adj sat		N Com co
	Position	poss	non-g		
	Metaphorical	pron	inherent		
mf	mf	mf	mf	mf	mb infl p1
Not	in	their	right	minds,	
c	s	c	c	c	
Den n	–	Den n	Den f	Den n	
–	–	–	Sp	Sp	
–	–	–	Ab	Conc 2	
				Body part meta-	
				phorical	
				Normal	
				Declarative	
				Complex	

	A							
	Circumstance							
Prep								
prep	art	Adj	N	Pron	Adv	dyn	Adj	N
dyn	def	ordi-	Com	III per	adjunct	transi-	poss	Com
accom-	cat	nal stat	Co	fem	focuss-	tional	pron	Co
paniment		non-g			ing	event		
		non-			mono-			
		inherent			addi-	trans		
					tive			

mf	mf	mf	mf	mb infl pl	mf	mf	mf mb infl III	mf	mb infl pl
With	the	other	deaths.	She,	too,		pursues	her	ends
s	s	c	c	c	c		c	c	c
–	–	Den n	con unf	Den n	Den n		Den n	Den n	Den n
–	–	–	Sp		–	–	Sp	–	Sp
–	–	–	Conc 1		–	–	Conc 2	–	Conc 2
–	–	–	calamity		–	–	business of life	–	body part business life
part ness of									

(Adjective Clause. Elliptical)

Adj	Conj		Noun Phrase mhq				
			mn		prep	mh	
Adj dyn grad in her	Conj compa-rison	art def Cata	N Com – Co		prep genitive	Adj dem	N Com Co
mf	mf	mf	mf	mb infl pl	mf	mf	mf
Brutal	as	the	stars		of	this	month,
c	s	s	c		s	c	c
Con unf	–	–	Den n		–	Den n	Den n
Sp	–	–	Sp		–	–	Sp
Conc	–	–	Conc 1		–	–	Conc 1
disposition		–	nature		–	–	nature

A
(Adv. Clause. Manner. Elliptical)

Noun Phrase
m m h q

m	m	h	Adj	Conj	N
					N
Adj Poss pron	Adj colour	N Com Co	pressure	Com-parison	Com m
mf	mf	mf	mf	mf	mf
Her	pale	head	heavy	as	metal
c	c	c	c	s	c
Den n	Con unf	Den N	Con unf	–	Den n
–	Sp	Sp	Sp	–	Gen

–	Conc 2 Colour abnormal	Conc 1 body part	Conc 2 weight (general)	–	Conc 1 geological material

Linguistic Pictures

1. *Sentence Pictures*

I. Simple, Complex, Complex,

II. Declarative. Declarative. Declarative.

III. A (V) S V A
A
S, A,
V, A
A
A. S, A, V Od
Od
A

2. *Clauses*

Now is the globe shrunk tight	main clause
Round the mouse's dulled wintering heart	main clause
Weasel and crow move through an outer darkness with the other deaths as if moulded in brass	dependent adv. clause (Elliptical)
Not in their right minds.	dependent adj. clause (Elliptical)
She, too, pursues her ends	main clause
Brutal as the stars of this month	dependent adj. clause (Elliptical)
Her pale head heavy as metal	dependent adv. clause (Elliptical)

3. *Word Classes*

Nouns (including pronouns)	:	15
Verbs:		
Finite	:	5 (including 1 aux)
non-finite	:	2

(including participial adjectives)		
Adjectives	:	11 (including 3 possessive and 1 ordinal)
Adverbs	:	3 (including 'not')
Articles	:	5
Prepositions	:	6
Conjunctions	:	5
Total	:	52

4. *Noun Phrases*

I. The globe	m h
the mouse's dulled wintering heart	m m m m h
weasel and crow	h + h
an outer darkness	m m h
their right minds	m m h
the other deaths	m m h
her ends	m h
the stars	m h (q)
this month	m h
her pale head	m m h

(The q where it has an ambiguous status has been left out.)

II. *Single Nouns*

brass

metal

5. *Semantic Pictures*

I. *Content and structure words*

c s s c c c
s s c c c c
c s c, s s c s c,
c s s c c
c s c c c
s s c c. c, c, c c c,
c s s c s c c
c c c c s c
c = 35

s = 17
Total = 52

II. *Content Words*

(a)	Denotative	Connotative
favourable	1	1
unfavourable		9
neutral	24	

Interpretation

Where the contemporary verse is concerned, we don't have to say much on the external context. The student is familiar with the world of today and shares with the poet the common concerns of humanity: he is liable to the same fears and hopes. The foreign student, however, is in need of specific information. Ted Hughes is a contemporary British poet. He was born in 1930. For brief periods he worked as a gardener and a night watchman. His poetry began appearing in the late 50's. He is greatly impressed by the vigour, ruthless dynamism and perseverance displayed by nature and animals.

The title refers to a plant which begins to show flowers while snow still lies on the ground and the rigours of winter are not yet over. It is better if the students carefully observe the plant or, at least, see a picture of it. It arouses a pleasant feeling with a tinge of hope. It should be noted that the title is all content—not a single empty element is added by way of inflexion. We have to contemplate a single plant: a generic item is viewed in its unique aspect like a proper noun. It is interesting to compare this with Wordsworth's, "The Daffodils". It is a concrete word comprehensible through the senses. In origin, however, the word consists of two free morphemes raising at the back of our mind some associations of the winter. We are orientated to nature.

There is no direct cohesion between the title and the first sentence which is split into two parts by verse division. The first verse seems to be a complete statement until we realise from the lack of any punctuation mark at the end that something more is to come. Let me digress here to say that we can read a poem aloud properly only after grasping its meaning. A wrong stressing, or pause or intonation may wreck the whole sentiment. "We have to pay attention to the meaning when stressing a sentence, for otherwise we may pass on our misunderstanding to everyone who hears us."[17] To resume the discussion, three things should be noticed in the first verse. With the dim awareness of cold, started up by the title, "shrunk tight" (both the words being mildly connotative unfavourable) seem to continue the strand at a deeper level and "the globe" used instead of "earth" gives the idea of an enclosing sphere. Thirdly, the subject and verb inversion with initial time adverb gives a serious mode to the thought. This structure (sometimes without inversion) is associated with sombre mood as in

Now is the midnight of the nations

in the war-poet, Percy Mackaye's terrible poem "Christmas: 1915", and

Now over the one half world
Nature seems dead

Macbeth, Act II Sc. 1

The second line consists of a preposition followed by a long noun phrase. "Wintering" removes the suspense as regards the thought and mood, although we still miss a direct link between the title and the first statement. I have marked "the" homophoric because it applies to "mouse" and not "heart"; this use makes us think of the whole species by visualizing an individual member. Verbality is at a low level; all the three verbs are process verbs and their active force has been further reduced by participial use. This device is responsible for an impression of slow internal activity. One thing more: the awkward rambling noun phrase reinforces the feeling of misery. The structure of noun phrase may become quite significant in poetry both for thought and feeling.[18]

The second sentence is a long and complex one with meaningful ambiguities. There is no article or adjective in the compound noun phrase in verse 3; this gives a touch of inclusiveness as in "the calamity hit man and beast". Although what follows the NP is an adverbial clause by function, by position, it looks like a q and this has a marked effect: we must conceive of weasel and crow in their brassy aspect. The separation of the verb by verse division makes the image quite distinct. "Move" is a dynamic verb, but it generally denotes involuntary transition, or displacement of inanimate objects: this accords well with the benumbed condition of the creatures and what follows in line 5: "Not in their right minds." The phrase following the verb in line 4 is truly adverbial. "Outer" points backward to inner darkness of the earth suggested in 11.1-2. "Globe" which is Concrete 1: contrasts with "darkness", Concrete 2: the earth is solid, the atmosphere is dry. The second sentence is very interesting: SAVAAA: the arrangement of sentence elements with their highly eccentric order are suggestive of the shattering effect of cold.

The grammatical sentence ends half way through in verse 6. This and the focusing adjunct "too" throw "she" onto the foreground. The personal pronoun accompanied by a very human expression "pursues her ends" flings a momentary surprise, but soon we perceive the anaphoric reference and with a thrill of discovery realise the main drift of the poem. "She" establishes direct cohesion with the title. Our sense of poetic register as well as parallelism with "move" (which is used in a literal sense): "Weasel and crow...move..., "She, too, pursues..." makes us suspect that "pursues her ends" may have a double meaning; literal and metaphorical. Now a lonely snowdrop is grimly set against the devastation of winter.

Line 7 confronts us with an ambiguity. Which word does the phrase modify? Is it an adverb or qualifier? In the proceeding portion "ends" is plural; we also have gathered that in a literal sense it suggests the flowers of the plant. Now in line 7 "stars" is also plural, moreover, it has a parallelism with flowers. I have therefore marked the expression as abjectival. "Brutal" in this connection is best interpreted to mean "harsh".

The last verse is semantically quite interesting: it raises the question of metaphor or semantic parallel. Archibald A. Hill has made a useful practical suggestion to identify semantic parallels,[19] although his two general principles stand in need of some further refining. His contention that each item added increases the significance of the semantic parallel is, I think, correct. "Pale" can be used for humans as well as colours and things. But when it is followed by "head", the metaphoric use is confirmed, it is further reinforced by the use of "heavy". We should, however, note that the word "head" is specific enough to settle the question and the other two words have a supporting function. The result is that we conceive of the snowdrop as a feminine individual burdened with misery. The struggle of beauty in a harsh milieu is presented in terms of a personified individual plant and this is essential for a proper experience of the poem. It would be interesting to compare this poem with Shakespeare's sonnet, "Since brass, nor stone, nor earth, nor boundless sea."

Once we have completed our reading, we sit back to cogitate upon the impact of the poem as a whole. First of all it comprises a cool, even statement without emotional flurry and rhetoric: there are no interrogative, exclamatory or imperative sentences and no strongly connotative words. But 9 out of 10 connotative words are unfavourable. The poem as a whole speaks of an unpleasant situation. The description is highly substantial or contentive: there are only 17 structural items out of 52, very few bound morphemes and a high degree of eclipsis. All these things define the condensed nature of the poem and account for its hard crystalline impact. As against this we can refer to Shakespeare's light-hearted description of winter characterised by a liberal use of structural words, loose structures and repetition:

When icicles hang by the wall
    And Dick the shepherd blows his nail,
And Tom bears logs into the hall,
    And milk comes frozen home in pail;
When blood is nipt, and ways be foul,
Then nightly sings the staring owl
    Tuwhoo!
Tuwhit! tuwhoo! A merry note

While greasy Joan doth keel the pot.

Lastly the poem is written in a nominal style. Most of the poem is in nominal groups. There are only 4 finite and 2 non-finite verbs (excluding 1 aux), of which only one, "pursue", is truly dynamic—even this is blunted by the use of "ends". The result is that the total impact creates a feeling of a fixed scene with slow mechanical activity. We can comprehend the affect of the poem better if we compare it with another treatment of winter in terms of energetic noisy activities. The poem is "Winter the Huntsman" by Osbert Sitwell:

Through his iron glades
Rides winter the Huntsman.
All colour fades
As his horn is heard sighing.

Far through the forest
His wild hooves crash and thunder
Till many a mighty branch
Is torn asunder.

References

1. Walter A. Davis, *The Act of Interpretation* (Chicago: The University of Chicago Press, 1978), 89.
2. Marjorie Boulton, *The Anatomy of Poetry* (1953; rpt. New Delhi: Kalyani Publishers, 1979), XII.
3. Alex Rodger, "Linguistics and the Teaching Literature" in *Applied Linguistics and the Teaching of English,* 2nd ed., ed. Hugh Fraser and W.R. O' Donnell (London: ELBS, 1973), 89.
4. I.A. Richards, *How to Read a Page,* 5th impr. (1943; London: Routledge and Kegan Paul, 1967), 14.
5. William C. Morse and G. Max Wingo, *Psychology and Teaching,* 3rd ed. (1962; Bombay: Taraporevala, 1970), 355.
6. Michael Roberts, ed. *The Faber Book of Modern Verse* (London: Faber, 1960), 3.
7. Winifred Nowottny, *The Language Poets Use* (London: The Athlone Press, 1962), 1.
8. J.A. Bright and G.P. McGregor, *Teaching English as a Second Language* (1970; London: ELBS, 1978), 222.
9. Robert Lado, *Language Teaching* (New York: McGraw Hill, 1964), 156.

10. Nils Erik Enkvist, John Spencer and Michael J. Gregory, *Linguistics and Style* (London: Oxford University Press U.P., 1964), 4.
11. M.A.K. Halliday, Angus McIntosh and Peter Strenvous, *The Linguistic Sciences and Language Teaching* (London: B.L.B.S., 1970), 246.
12. I.A. Richards, *Principles of Literary Criticism,* Indian rpt. (1925; Bombay: Allied Publishers), 88.
13. C. Day Lewis, "The Poet's way of knowledge" in *Perspectives in Poetry,* ed. by James L. Calderwood and Harod E. Toliver (New York: Oxford University Press, 1963), 302.
14. M.A.K. Halliday, "Descriptive Linguistics in Literary Studies", In *Patterns of Language: Papers in General, Descriptive and Applied Linguistics,* by Angus McIntosh and M.A.K. Halliday (London: Longmans, 1966), 60.
15. Marjorie Boulton, *The Anatomy,* 107-08.
16. I.A. Richards, "Poetic Process and Literary Analysis" in *Style in Language,* ed. by Thomas A. Sebeok (Cambridge Mass: The M.T.I. Press, 1960), 13.
17. Morjorie Boulton, *The Anatomy,* 19.
18. S.K. Singh, "A Linguistic Study of John Donne's Major Poems" (Unpublished Ph.D. Dissertation, Magadh University, 1976), 410.
19. Archibald, A. Hill, "Principles Governing Semantic Parallels" In *Applied English Linguistics,* ed. H.B. Allen (1958; Delhi: Amrind Publishing Co., 1971), 506-09.

Part - III

Neurogrammar, Lexicography and Equivalence in Translation

Neurogrammar

16

Neuro-linguistics has made considerable progress in recent decades. With the introduction of brain imaging, neuro-linguists are able to study the activity of the brain during speech production and reception. But the problem is far from having been solved. Earlier it was thought that two areas in the left hemisphere are responsible for speech activity. But now it is realized that many areas and points in the brain become active to accomplish the task of speech reception and speech production.

Still it is better and more scientific to trace the steps and processes that occur in the brain when we are constructing the grammar of a language. This will check a lot of unnecessary philosophising and logical modeling that generally accompanies the proposal for a new grammar. When we examine the history of grammars we find that many speculative designs have proved to be false or unhelpful.

A better way is to construct a grammar in accordance with the activities taking place in the brain itself. Broadly speaking it is still true that the two main areas of language activities are situated in the left hemisphere of the brain. Wernicke's area is situated towards the back near the left ear. This area receives the language input from outside through the ear. It seems that the words in the input are stored in a coded form in Wernicke's Area. Studies of Wernicke's Aphasia have shown that the patients suffering from a lesion in this area are unable to find the right words needed in their sentences. This means that the structures which they are able to use correctly are the responsibility of another area of the brain. Those who suffer injury in the other area namely, Broca's Area, are unable to construct sentences. This means that the structures abstracted from the input are stored and activated in Broca's area.

It should be noted that there is a channel of nerve fibers connecting these two areas; most probably, as suggested by Chomsky, the grammar is abstracted in the brain itself and, as Chomsky further suggests, the structures thus acquired are used to form new sentences.

It has been noted that those suffering damage in Broca's area are also unable to use the structure words, which, it may be noted, are actually part of the structure or form rather than content. The Broca's area activates complete sentences and issues instructions, to the speech apparatus for their production. Roughly we may say that Wernicke area is responsible for the reception of the speech and Broca area for the completion and production of speech. In grammatical terms we may conceive of this picture in the following way:

If Wernicke's area is responsible for all the words, then the sentence, 'The boys like the mangoes' will have the following structure:

The boy—like the mango:

In this case all the words are supplied by the Wernicke area. Only inflections are given by the Broca's Area.

On the other hand, if Wernicke area supplies only the content words then the picture will be as follows:

—boy—like—mango—.

In this case structure words as well as the sentence patterns, are supplied by the Brocka's area. The dashes represent supplied by the structural items supplied by the Broca's Area.

Now what are the implications of this brain activity for constructing a grammar: (1) It seems that the brain is able to recognize and store separately function words and structure words. Our grammar must make this classification clearly and show how the list of content word is open ended whereas that of the structure words is closed for every language. Secondly structure word should form part of the sentence pattern. We have no certain evidence regarding the complex process of transformation involving deletion, movement and addition.

In the above discussion we have done no more than indicating the directions in which our grammar-making should proceed. This is necessarily tentative and most elementary proposal which we hope would be considered and investigated in future research.

Modern Trends in Lexicography

17

It may be stated at the outset that modern dictionaries (especially English dictionaries) have become deeply involved with the needs and interests of the user and consumer. This new orientation has led to certain well-marked innovations in lexicographical techniques and methods of presentation. On the whole, the scope of lexicography has undergone vast expansion.

One of the most important innovations has been the adding of usage and subject labels, where usage covers both the stylistic range from formal to colloquial and situational meaning in terms of positive and negative connotation which is crucial in actual communication. What can happen in the absence of such knowledge is well illustrated by a legal case registered in America. The matter was reported in the *New York World* of January 19, 1913. A young woman complained that one Starner had insulted her publicly by accosting her with 'Hello chicken'. The accused requested the magistrate to consult a dictionary because he felt he had not done anything improper. The Magistrate took out an old edition of Webster which contained the following entry:

Chicken—The young of various birds, a child, a young woman.

Starner was discharged. After relating this incident in his paper titled, 'A Point of Lexicographical Method' Daniel Cook

---

Originally appeared in *Bhashacinatana,* Vol. 2, 2007.

underlined "the widespread and long-standing inadequacy in the treatment of terms that are actually available only for an extremely limited range that are actually available only for an extremely limited range of contexts (Allen, ed. 1967: 450-51). In practical use of language it is very important to know whether a word has a positive or negative connotation and what is the degree or level of its negativity, this is the reason why a modern dictionary makes a liberal use of usage labels and specified situational meanings where necessary. Daniel Cook in the article cited above examines various dictionaries until he reaches the second edition of Webster's NID published in 1934 which lists the relevant meaning of chicken: 5 Slang 'a young woman of easy familiarity' (Allen 455).

It must be noted here that word meaning is subject to change and that slang is the most volatile part of vocabulary. Therefore, for contemporary usage, a recent standard dictionary needs to be consulted. However, in modern lexicography and subject labels have become well-established in practice and every dictionary employ scores of such labels. The significance of this feature will become quite clear if we look up some words in a few pocket and desk dictionaries (the types that are most widely and quite frequently consulted) citing only the labeled meanings and spelling of each label in full:

Word	Pocket Oxford (1992)	The Cassell Pocket English Dictionary (1991)	The New Penguin (2000)	Webster's (1987)
aberration	(Astronomical) apparent displacement of a celestial body	(No label) the difference between the true and observed position of heavenly body	In astronomy, a small periodic change of apparent position in celestial bodies due to the combined effect of the speed of light and the motion of the observer	(astron.) the angular difference between the true and apparent position. (optics) the failure of reflected or refracted light

(Contd...)

dad	Colloquial, father	(No label) a child's name for father	informal an affectionate name for one's father	(popular) father of
culture vulture	Person eager for cultural pursuits	(Coll., often derogatory) a person avidly interested in arts	Humorous a person who has an avid sometimes uncritical, interest in culture	(the word not given)
baby	slang sweet heart	(colloquial) a girl; a pet project	Slang an affectionate form of address for a person esp. a girl or woman	(the meaning under reference not given)
cow	derogatory slang woman	(sl. Derogatory) a woman	Informal, a woman, esp. one who is unpleasant in some way	(the meaning under reference not given)
nigger	Offensive, black or dark-skinned person	(offensive) a negro (offensive) one of any dark-skinned people	(offensive or derogatory) a black person esp. one of African race	(Offensive term of contempt) a Negro
morn	(Poetical morning)	(poet) morning	(literary) morning	(rhetorical) morning
commence	(formal) begin	(No label) to start; to begin	to start or begin something	v.t. to begin v.i. to have a beginning
nigh	Archaic or dialect, near	(No label) near	Archaic, near in place, time of relation	(archaic) near

Modern linguistic investigation of language structure has clearly demonstrated that there is a close interrelationship between meaning, grammar and use and mere knowledge of word meaning is of no use in linguistic communication. A.S. Hornby was among the first to integrate grammar as an essential component of the lexical entry. His *Advanced Learner's Dictionary* is now an indispensable resource for all non-native learners of English. Although this work cannot be classed with general dictionaries, the trend of incorporating essential grammatical information has caught on and been further methodized in general lexicography.

Before modernization of lexicography, the dictionary usually indicated to which part of speech a word belonged and if it was a verb, whether it was transitive or intransitive. Nowadays, a modern dictionary would provide a lot more information at the grammatical level. Here are some examples chosen from the dictionaries already mentioned. *Abase* is a verb, also used reflexively; *abashed* is a predicative adjectives; *blues* in the sense of bout of depression is preceded by the and treated as plural, while in the sense of melancholic music it is preceded by *the* but treated as singular; *averse* is predicative adjective usually followed by *to* (Pocket Oxford). Modern dictionaries use *somebody* and *something* to indicate whether the object of a verb or complement of an adjective is + human, – human or ± human. *Aware* is often followed by *of* and it means 'conscious of something'; *confuse* is a transitive verb meaning 'to bewilder or purplex (somebody)'; *reincarnate* is a transitive verb usually used in passive. (The New Penguin), *Advanced Learner's Dictionary* (OUP) provides a lot more grammatical information. Some other publications have also issued Advanced Learner's Dictionaries. The one by Cambridge University Press supplies substantial structural information, such as, + that, + obj. +v. ing, + object + Adj., etc.

As we move higher to concise, desk and full dictionaries, we become aware of the other roles of the lexicographer. The matter has been discussed by Arthur Delbridge and P.H. Peters in an article humorously titled, 'Dictator, Gatekeeper, Tally Clerk or Harmless Drudge?' in Burton, T.L. and Burton, Jill, (1988). Drudgery, most certainly, is the common factor in all lexicographical work, but the first three roles have definite purposes and procedures: the first focuses on authoritative meaning, the second is chiefly concerned with barring the entry of disreputable and ephemeral items and the third concentrates on the purely descriptive aspect.

The standard editions of Oxford, Webster and Chambers scrupulously adhere to the first two norms, but descriptivism has been expanding its scope throughout lexicographic enterprise.

Two hallmarks of modern lexicography are user friendliness and descriptivism involving a host of new techniques and devices. Some easily noticeable ones will be discussed here with examples:

1. Structural items are explained with the help of illustrations. In *Pocket Oxford* there is a long articles on *as* as an adverb and conjunction containing illustrations like *am as tall as he, as recently as last week, came early, so as to meet us.* The article also includes such combinations as, as far, as from, as if, as though, as it were. *Concise Oxford* gives its meanings and uses as adverb, conjunction and preposition without any examples. *The New Penguin,* enters the word separately with illustrative sentences in each case.
2. Usage Notes on Grammar are added. The Reader's Digest, *Great Illustrated Dictionary* (in two volumes) discusses the term with examples and adds the following usage note:

   In positive comparisons, the double use of *as* is required: *He's as tall as I am.* In negative comparisons, traditional grammar prescribes so... (He's not so tall as I am), but as...as is still widely used. Several *as* constructions are potentially ambiguous. A sentence such as *He came as I was leaving* could be interpreted to mean either "he came at the time as I left" or "He came because I was leaving". A similar ambiguous case is "He likes her as much as Jim", which could mean as much as "he like Jim" or "as much as Jim likes her"! This prompts some speakers to use I in place of me in such sentences as He likes her as much as I (do), He likes her as much as (he likes) me.
3. Such usage notes, not only on grammar but also on meaning and other issues, have become a common feature in modern dictionaries. A few examples will be in order:

   (a) The use of aggravate in sense 2 is regarded by some people as incorrect, but it is common in informal use (*Pocket Oxford*).

   (b) Words for lavatory constitute one of the most changeable areas of vocabulary, as people search for the most polite or neutral expression. *Loo* is a recent development in British English, used widely but only informally. *Lavatory* and *toilet* are both acceptable in middle-class usage, but the latter is more frequently used... (*Great Illustrated*; 999)

4. In addition to usage notes, *The New Penguin* supplies, what it calls 'Editorial notes'. The purpose of this innovation is explained in the preface:

   To go behind the facts of words' meanings to explore the concepts behind them, we have invited a range of distinguished writers and academics to write miniature essays on topics that relate to their work: noteworthy contribution include David Crystal on the alphabet and language, Richard Dawkins on Darwinism and evolution, and Catherine Belsey on deconstruction and formalism, all terms that threated to burst the bounds that dictionaries conventionally impose upon them.

5. This dictionary also offers interesting notes on word history. Here is an example: relating to *dunce:*

   From the name of John Duns Scotus, d. 1308, Scots theologian whose once accepted writings were ridiculed in the 16th cent. Followers of Duns Scotus, known as Dunsmen or Dunses, were regarded as dull pedants, and from this the word *dunce* came to mean 'slow learner'.

We shall have to say a little more on this topic when we take up the question of word etymology. But continuing the present discussion, let us mention some specific user-friendly devices. The eighth edition of *Pocket Oxford Dictionary* states in the Preface that it "takes even further the aims of the seventh edition towards making information easier to find and easier to understand". The policy of denesting is continued. In other dictionaries also we find the same trend. *The New Penguin*, for example, gives *adapt, adaptation* and *adapter* as separate entries. Also, where a difference of meaning is noticed, the same form is entered separately under superscripts 1, 2, 3, etc. We also find that where a word with a prefix or suffix has a distinct meaning or linguistic identity, it is entered independently, e.g. *recover* and *re-cover*.

Dr. Samuel Johnson was the first lexicographer who supported meanings of words with citations in his *A Dictionary of the English Language 1755*. His *Dictionary* supplied thousands of quotations illustrating the use of words, so that, as Johnson remarked in his Preface, where his own explanations are inadequate 'the sense may easily be collected entirely from the example' (Baugh 1978: 328). Following the lead given by Johnson, the traditional dictionaries drew their citations from the works of eminent writers, mostly of literature, such as Shakespeare, Milton, Dryden, Swift.

But now, there is a radical shift. With emphasis being laid on communication and contemporary discourse and with the facility of electronic recording and computer processing, the basis has shifted from literary works to samples of language actually employed in real communicative situations. For English, a number of corpora consisting of millions of words and sentences have already been built and are made available to lexicographers. As David Crystal has remarked "compiling a corpus is very different from the traditional practices of citation-gathering or word watching" which have guided work on dictionaries since the time of Dr. Johnson (1995: 438).

Illustrative examples in the *The New Penguin* come from literature as well as modern corpus, and the citations cover a wide range, as in, "beggar.... It beggars description". The sentence, although in modern form reminds us of Enobarbus' appreciation of Cleopatra, "fashion is really about being naked" Vivienne Westwood. "hoax.... The bomb warning turned out to be a hoax". The editors of *Concise Oxford* "have made use of huge amounts of corpus material and other computerized evidence, including 100 millions word British National Corpus, and the citation database of the Oxford World Reading Programme, currently standing at around 48 million words and growing at a rate of around 5 million words per year* (Preface). A couple of examples will be enough to support this statement: 'dab'...she puts a dab of perfume behind her ears"; throng....'a crowd thronged the station'.

Modern lexicographers are quite particular about pronunciation and most dictionaries provide a chart of symbols and marks in terms of which each word is transcribed. Most lexicographers now take cognizance of phonemicity and base their transcription on actual pronunciation rather than questionnaires, and the sources have also changed. Description of phonemes and the electronic revolution have profoundly affected the sources and manners of speech recording and its representation in a dictionary. Albert H. Marckwardt comments on the radical shift made in *Webster's Third New International Dictionary* (published in 1961) owing to the introduction of the microphone:

> Where Webster Second had attempted a sampling, by means of written questionnaires, of the pronunciation of persons who did a considerable amount of public speaking, the Webster Third staff turned its attention directly to the language itself rather than to opinion about it. They listened to radio, television, and recordings; to speech in all parts of the country in all types of situations.
>
> (Marckwardt, A.H. in Allen, H.B., ed. 1967: A83)

At present, there are two major systems of phonetic representation in dictionaries with some unidirectional interpenetration. The one followed by the Oxford group of dictionaries uses the IPA symbols with slight adaptation here and there, the other employed chiefly by Webster dictionaries is a kind of re-spelling which depends on the English alphabet. The second system is easier to follow but is rather loose and liable to create some confusion. The IPA-based system is more scientific and ensures greater accuracy. However, some American dictionaries can capture certain minor details which go unrepresented in the IPA based framework. It would be interesting to compare a few items as found in Reader's Digest *Great Illustrated Dictionary* and *Oxford Concise,* although the latter addresses itself only to the pronunciation difficulties of the native speakers of English.

In fact the question of native speaker and standard pronunciation of English has become quite problematic after globalization of English, and the resulting complexity is reflected in the mixed and generalized systems that are being tried in English lexicography. *Concise Oxford* (1999) uses |a| instead of |æ| as in cat, |ɛ :| instead of |eə| as in hair |ΔI| instead of |ai| as in *my*. No doubt, the pronunciation of vowels, particularly, is also undergoing change, as is quite natural.

Stress marking in dictionaries is also subject to some variation. We can identify three points. American dictionaries, generally place the mark immediately after the stressed syllable or put it on the vowel of the stressed syllable. In Oxford dictionaries the mark appears just before the stressed syllable. In every case, for proper stressing, the whole word must be re-pronounced.

It should not be surprising that in this age of descriptivism, etymology is placed on the back-burner. Generally, etymology, where given, receives very little space; *The Cassell Pocket* (1991) has dispensed with it altogether, on the other hand *The New Penguin* offers etymology as well as (in some selected cases) word history.

Although etymology has lost ground in the sphere of practical utility, it retains its appeal as an interesting subject like folk tales and antiques and as proper study in historical linguistics. This is attested by the appearance or re-issue of such titles as *Skeat's The Concise Dictionary of English Etymology* and E. Funk's *Word Origins*. But subject dictionaries operate on a different level and they have a great utility for the specialist. That is why there has been a tremendous boom in such publications. These two kinds of dictionaries, being specialized lexicons lie beyond the pale of my present concern; I shall not, therefore explore these areas any further, they, however, offer ample scope for further lexicographical research.

But we cannot ignore reference dictionaries which are very useful to the general reader, whose reading experience requires something more than word meaning and a little of what is found in a voluminous encyclopedia. As Marckwardt reports, one cause of dissatisfaction with Webster Third (1961) was that it dropped the items of general information. "Think, if you can, complains Wilson Follet, of an unabridged dictionary from which you cannot learn who Mark Twain was, or what were the names of the apostles, or that Virgin was Mary, the mother of Jesus of Nazareth, or what and where the district of Columbia is" (in Allen, H.B. 1967: 481). As many dictionaries will readily show, the encyclopedic matter is not an essential part of a dictionary, yet it is a desirable and most welcome feature and many Websters and *Reader's Digest, The Great Illustrated Dictionary* include it. Another solution is a reference dictionary which combines word meaning and reference and the name that comes to mind readily is *The Oxford Reference Dictionary,* which states in the beginning that it "is designed to function both as a dictionary and as a concise encyclopedia" (Preface). The Dictionary does include entries on Mark Twain, the apostles, and the virgin, but Columbia is not important enough to deserve a place.

Finally, I must mention a recent development in lexicography which addresses itself to the most important and difficult problem of the active user, one who wishes to speak and write a language (English in this case) correctly and appropriately—finding the right word or cluster of words for an idea present in the user's mind. Such works are commonly known as 'reverse dictionary' and we can gain a better idea about such works by glancing through *Reader's Digest Reverse Dictionary* (1989). In place of a preface or introduction, we have an article entitled 'From the idea to the world', which begins:

> Everyone has experienced the frustration of mislaying a familiar word. You know what you want to say; you know that the precise word exists that will enable you to say it; and you know that you know this word.... But when you reach for it it's not there. That's when the pantomime of exasperation begins: you snap your fingers, you frown, you rummage about in your mental attic, you say "It's on the tip of my tongue" or "What's that word-oh, you know." But the word, hovering just out of reach, continues to elude and tantalise you. Psychologists studying this phenomenon

> compare it to being on the brink of a sneeze. Anticipation...concentration...and—frustration. What's needed, so to speak, is a pinch of snuff. *The Reverse Dictionary* provides one. It's linguistic snuffbox, helping to release the pent-up sneeze. The relief it affords should be considerable.
>
> As we read on, we learn that the familiar "Cue word" leads to the mind-puzzling "target word" in any of three different ways: through definition, through a chart of terms or through an illustration. In course of reading the definition of *ability* we come across *caliber, acumen* and *potential,* any of which could be the word we were searching (11). For *abbey* we have to examine the illustration on page 12 and for *non-agenarian* we must see the chart on AGES OF MAN. (17)

Longman's Essential Activator (1998) also helps us to put our ideas into words, but it has a recognizably pedagogical purpose and takes advantage strategies of linguistic communication and of lexical sets, and semantic fields—all these topics are relevant where the aim is to help the user find the right word and use it appropriately. This new kind of dictionary is based on a corpus and includes essential grammar, word banks, help boxes and situational language samples often found in communication.

When we examine the roles linguistic communication plays in the modern scenario (often called 'the age of communication') we can fully understand the new trends and experimentation in lexicography. It can also be reasonably expected that the vigorous activity being witnessed in lexicographical publication and research is likely to proliferate in the foreseeable future. In this process, the new techniques and methods that will certainly spring up from time to time will require close analysis and study from lexicographical and pedagogical points of view.

Works Cited

Allen, Harold Byron. *Applied English Linguistics*. 2nd ed. New Delhi: Oxford ed. IBH, 1967.

Allen, Robert, Consultant Ed. *The Penguin English Dictionary*. (Indian rprt.) New Delhi: Penguin India, 2000.

Baugh. A.C. *A History of the English Language*. (Indian rprt.) Bombay: Allied, 1978.

Burton, T.L. and Burton, Jill. *Lexicographical and Linguistic Studies: Essays in Honour of G.W. Turner*. Cambridge: D.S. Brewer, 1988.

Cook, Daniel. "A Point of Lexicographical Method" in Allen, 1967.

Crystal, David. *The Cambridge Encyclopedia of the English Language*. New York: CUP, 1999.

Delbridye, Arthur and Peters, P.H. "Dictator, Gatekeeper, Tally Clerk and Harmless Drudge?" in Burtone, T.L. and Burton, Jill, 1988.

Funk, Wilfred. *Word Origins*, Indian ed. New Delhi: Goyl Saab, 1988.

Gillard, Patrick, Sr. Com. Ed. *Advanced Learners Dictionary*. London: CUP, 2003.

Ilson, Robert Consel. Ed. *Great Illustrated Dictionary* (2 vols.). London: Reader's Digest Association, 1984.

Joyce M. Hawkins, Ed. *The Oxford Reference Dictionary*, Oxford: OUP, 1986.

Kahn. J.E. *Reverse Dictionary*. London: Reader's Digest Association, 1989.

Kirkpatrick, Betty, Ed. *The Cassell Pocket English Dictionary*. London: Arrow Books, 1991.

Longman. *Essential Activator*. Indian rprt. Delhi: Longman, 1998.

Marckwardt, A.H. *The New Webster Dictionary: A Critical Appraisal* in Allen H.B., 1967.

Pearsall, Judy. *The Concise Oxford Dictionary*. Indian Ed. New Delhi: OUP, 1999.

Skeat, Walter W. *The Concise Dictionary of Etymology*, Hertfordshire: Wordsworth, 1993.

The New Lexicon Webster's Dictionary. New York: Lexicon Publications, 1988.

Thomson, Delia, Ed. *The Pocket Oxford Dictionary of Current English* (Indian ed.). New Delhi: OUP, 1996.

Wehmeier, Sally, Ed. *Advanced Learner's Dictionary*. 6th ed. London: OUP, 2000.

The Question of Equivalence in Translation

18

Most theorists agree that equivalence is a major factor in translation. But it is very difficult to fix the parameters of equivalence. What ought to be clear is the fact that the linguistic matter of the source language is carried over in the field of another language or target language. But it is not very clear what exactly is to be transferred in a translation. We know that a piece of a language has both content and form. The basic element in content is the meaning of the expression, but content includes many other important factors such as cultural code, context and situation in which the utterances are spoken. That is why some theorists prefer the term *message* rather than *meaning*. It is the message not simply the semantic content which is transferred from one language to another. As far as the linguistic structure is concerned we can think of phonological, morphological, syntactic and semantic equivalence.

When we take into account the whole spectrum of linguistic scope it is clear that total equivalence in any translation is almost impossible to achieve. What we generally get in a translation is the meaning of words and sentences. Since every language has a unique phonological system, phonological equivalence cannot be achieve. For example, how can we transfer the sound-effect of the following line:

चली धार धुधकार धरा दिशि कार्टात कावा

Or

ठुठुकि चलत रामचन्द्र बाजत पैंजनियाँ
किलकिलाप उठत धाय गिरत भूमि लटपटाप

In the same way morphology and syntax are also unique. Latin is a V language, English is SVO and Hindi SOV. There are many other differences when we go to the details of the structure of these languages. These components are also difficult to transfer. But these things could be a part of a translator's ambition and he could achieve a limited amount of success in transferring the phonetic, morphological and syntactic patterns in terms of the structure of the target language. Once I attempted a Hindi translation of a small portion of Pearl S. Buck's autobiography, called *My Several Worlds*. This portion was concerned with India. My ambition was to convey an impression through my translation that the original writer was an English lady whose mother tongue was English, not Hindi. For this purpose I manipulated the normal syntactic patterns of Hindi language:

भारत हमेशा मेरे जीवन की पृष्ठभूमि का अंग रहा है किन्तु उसके पहले कभी भी मैंने उसको समूचा तथा प्रत्यक्ष नहीं देखा था। फिर भी जो कहानियाँ मेरे बाल्यकाल में हमारे भारतीय घरेलू चिकित्सक तथा उसकी पत्नी ने मुझे सुनाई, वह मेरे उगते सपनों में गुंथ गई थीं और उस देश के बारे में जो भी मुझे प्राप्त हो सका मैं पहले ही पढ़ चुकी थी। बौद्धदर्शन तथा महात्मा बुद्ध के जीवन-चरित्र के माध्यम से उस देश के बारे में मैं अपने पिता से जान चुकी थी। भारत का प्रतिकूल रूप भी मैंने देखा था, शंघाई स्थित ब्रितानी कन्सेशन पर पगड़ीधारी सिक्ख सिपाही था, जिसे भाग्यहीन चीनी रिक्शेवाले को पीटने में कोई संकोच नहीं होता था यदि उसने यातायात में अवरोध किया अथवा पगड़ीधारियों की दबंग आज्ञाओं का उल्लंघन किया। भारत एकरस नहीं था। और युवा भारतीयों से मैं इंग्लैण्ड के उपनिवेशी साम्राज्य के बारे में उसकी कुछ बुराइयों और अच्छाइयों के बारे में जान चुकी थी।

I also wrote the following sentences which appear to be deviant from the point of view of Hindi syntax.

- चीन और भारत एक दूसरे से इतने असमान हैं जितने कि दो देश हो सकते हैं।
- इस प्रकार चीनियों ने अपने खून तक में अपने सभी आक्रामकों को स्वीकार कर लिया है जहाँ तक आक्रामकों ने स्वयं को करने दिया।

- उसके बजाय उसने जातियों को अलग-अलग हालांकि अपने सम्पूर्ण का एक भाग रहने दिया है।
- धर्म भारतीय जीवन में सदा उपस्थित रहता है, अपने उत्कृष्ट तथा निकृष्ट दोनों पहलुओं में, क्योंकि वहाँ, जैसी सभी जगह, धर्मान्धता पाप तक पहुँच जाती है।

Postmodern theorists take an unfavourable view of translation. They hold that every translation is not only incomplete but it also involves motivated interpretation; translation according to them is not an innocent activity. It is involved with power structure, cultural code, sexual politics, etc. There are three factors in any translation; language, period and the translator. One can never get rid of these factors completely. It is, therefore, believed that translation is never objective. I wish to say that there is an ability of the human mind which is totally ignored by the postmodern relativists. The translator must show his fidelity to the text. And it is not impossible to achieve, a measure of objective translation when this focus on the text is carefully maintained. In the modern global scenario translation is a very important cultural agency. And however insufficient, it certainly satisfies the needs of the modern man. Because viewed in a larger perspective, translation is not confined only to a linguistic text. Semiotically speaking, modern lifestyle involves translation of so many codes—cultural, social, ethical, sartorial, etc.